W9-BXT-286

We Are All Close

A learned man who partook of the Sabbath meal at the home of Rabbi Baruch ben Jehiel (1757—1810) of Medzibezh (Poland, until 1793; thereafter Russia), grandson of the Ba'al Shem Tov, said to his host:

"Let me now hear you talk of your doctrine; you speak so beautifully."

"May I be struck dumb ere I speak beautifully!" was Rabbi Baruch's reply; and he said nothing more.

The conversation of authors is not so good as might be imagined; but, such as it is (and with rare exceptions), it is better than any other. — William Hazlitt

HAIM CHERTOK

We

CONVERSATIONS

Are All

WITH ISRAELI

Close

WRITERS

Fordham University Press / New York

FOR MARCIA

© Copyright 1989 by Fordham University

All rights reserved.

LC 89-80058

ISBN 0-8232-1223-8

Designed by Richard Hendel.

Printed in the United States of America

Contents

Introduction

This representative sampling of conversations with Israeli writers stretches from November 1983, when I met with novelist Aharon Appelfeld at the Café Atara in Jerusalem, to March 1988, when I spoke with short-story writer Yael Medini at her home in Ramat Gan—a span of nearly five years. The notion that English-speaking readers might be interested in eavesdropping on the table talk of Israeli writers was initially suggested by Mitchell Cohen, at the time editor of the *Jewish Frontier*, the Labor Zionist bi-monthly in New York. In fact, in a variety of forms, fully half of these verbal encounters first made their appearance in the pages of the *Frontier*.

Choosing which writers to approach turned out to be very largely a matter of chance. In 1982 the English-language daily *The Jerusalem Post* printed my appreciative notice of Appelfeld's novel *The Age of Wonders*. With it as my calling card, I painlessly arranged a meeting with the author a year-and-a-half thereafter. In fact, most of the ensuing meetings were to be with writers whose books it fell my lot to review either in the *Post* or in the Jerusalem-based cultural quarterly *Ariel*.

It might be well for the reader to bear in mind several factors that doubtless affected the tone of these encounters. First, with just a single exception, I did not talk with any writer whose work I do not genuinely admire. Moreover, with those writers considerably older than I, I find that I tended rather naturally to assume a deferential stance. Consequently, though on occasion I did deliberately choose to be provocative, both the selective procedure itself and the given situation served to blunt any inclination toward visceral confrontation.

Three additional matters pertaining to these particular 18 figures deserve to be noted: when my primary intent was to see these pieces published in English-language journals, I chose to meet with Israeli writers in whom I thought American readers were likely to have a prior interest. However, once it was plain that these conversations were likely to comprise *We Are All Close,* I consciously set out to include some of Israel's younger or less well-known quality writers. My purpose, obviously, was to present a fairer balance, a more general cross-section of Israeli writers.

A collateral effect of aiming for balance, however, is that I have scanted many talented, established Israeli authors whom one might well have expected to see included in such a collection, people of the stature of Amalia Kahana-Carmon, Yoram Kaniuk, Hayim Guri, S. Yizhar, and Aharon Megged. Suffice it to say that Hebrew literature is currently enjoying a period of unparalleled fruition and that a companion volume presenting writers not included in *We Are All Close* but of comparable quality could easily be conceived. (*Why* Israeli culture should now, in such a difficult time, be so luxuriant is one of the matters several of the writers touch upon.)

Finally, I deliberately included a few Israeli writers who are fellow *olim* (honorific for immigrants to Israel) from English-speaking countries and who continue to write in English. My feeling was that their experience would be of particular interest to readers of the book.

All but three of the writers I wanted to meet and record made themselves available. And one of these, novelist Aliza Amir, was willing enough, but she resides on a kibbutz on the Lebanese border. Twice distance and circumstance foiled our planned rendezvous.

As my interviewing "strategy" evolved with experience, it was to give my respondents their philosophical, literary, personal, or political head as far as seemed profitable. I myself generally struck certain chords: Zionism, Palestinians, Jewishness,

Diaspora, translation, other authors. With increasing frequency, I refer back to the views expressed by writers from earlier interviews. This has tended, I think, to generate a lively, natural kind of running dialogue among the respondents, and the discerning reader will detect among them areas of agreement and discord. Indeed, though such was not a primary intention, I believe that *We Are All Close* succeeds in conveying the general atmosphere and central concerns of the Israeli intellectual community in the Eighties.

On rereading, the encounters seem to me quite various. Some writers were inclined to talk a great deal about their own lives and experiences; others eschewed anything that smacked of the personal. With the former, I generally tried to encourage expression of their views on public matters; with the latter, to reveal something of their inner lives. Sometimes I think I even succeeded. My own part in these conversations varies considerably for reasons, I am sure, readers will themselves readily discern. I did not fail to make an attempt—usually all too transparent—to cajole or tempt each writer to talk about his or her own work or craft. Few, on these most intimate grounds, were especially forthcoming. Nonetheless, I have recorded a portion of the writers' generally charming evasiveness in the face of my squirrelly persistence.

I notice that I have interchangeably designated these meetings "conversations" and "interviews." In fact, some of them tended toward the former mode, others toward the latter. In every case I tried to follow the lead of the writer, to let him or her clear the most suitable path. To this end, I have preserved a generous portion of preliminary small talk, interlinear chat, and the mise en scène. My primary aim was not to record anecdotes or enshrine set-piece opinions. Rather it was to capture to the greatest possible extent a sense of the writer's personality, the special flavor of each respondent's style, voice, and presence.

I perceived my own real target most clearly when I met with

Anton Shammas, the talented Israeli Arab who writes in Hebrew
(and currently lives in the United States). His memoir *Arabesques*
had recently been published by Harper and Row. He was tired
and obviously did not really want to be "interviewed." Nevertheless, we talked amiably for an hour over beers at a café in Jerusalem, and Shammas was expansive about a variety of subjects
that included Arabic poetry, the Sistine Chapel, the problems of
literary translation, and his year in Iowa City. I particularly re-
frained from impinging on personal or political matters. Still,
it was plain that what emerged was just the sort of unrestrained
verbal flow issuing from authentic authorial personality that I
was aiming for.

Immediately after Shammas departed, I transcribed from
memory a detailed account of our conversation and mailed it to
him. Painlessly (I thought) "interviewed" in spite of himself, his
reaction startled me. He preferred that I should not publish the
record of his table talk. It was not that my account was flawed.
(On the contrary, he complimented its accuracy.) Nor that it
contained any personal revelations or embarrassing material.
And it was not that he had been traduced. Rather it was that he
felt that his remarks were too superficial and ill-considered;
therefore, he would not want his name attached to them. To no
avail was my subsequent effort to persuade him that his "interview" served my purpose admirably, that he was doing himself a
disservice. Obviously, I still regret his decision.

I find that I have already referred to this volume as offering a
representative "cross-section" of Israeli writers and, by extension, of the Israeli intelligentsia during our recent period. Indeed, it is my hope that even readers with close acquaintance
with the Israeli literary or cultural scene of the mid-'80s would
gain heightened familiarity with this special, very influential
community. At second blink, however, it is plain how remarkably revealing my remark actually is. In the first place, with the
defection of Shammas, this compilation includes not one Israeli
Arab writer!

Equally remarkable, I am abashed to point out that every one of the 18 writers who appear in this collection is of Northern European or North American, *Ashkenazi* background. Not a one can point to roots in the *Sephardi* Jewish communities of Southern Europe or the Arab countries. And yet such is the literary culture of contemporary Israel that, though of course exceptions could be cited—novelists Amnon Shamosh and Sammy Michael, poet Ronnie Someck, a number of others—my claim to being representative can justly stand. To all intents and purposes, Israeli literary culture today is not only predominantly leftist but wholly dominated by *Ashkenazim.*

Some technical matters: in recording the remarks of these writers, I did not employ any mechanical device. I preferred instead, usually on the following day, to reconstruct each conversation with the aid of close notes and a reasonably sound memory. Such is the run of my own temperament and, it was my feeling, such would probably also be more congenial for the respondents as well. I think that in this I was generally correct.

I have striven both for an accurate rendering of the authors' actual words *and* for the effect of verisimilitude. As any dramatist could testify, these aims are not identical. These accounts, therefore, are not exact transcriptions of every utterance. Furthermore, several of these accounts—Appelfeld's, Amichai's, one or two of the others'—incorporate a modest amount of material drawn from several conversations. In sum, while there are no "additions," the text has been edited with transpositions and elisions.

The factor of language itself must needs be mentioned. For my convenience, most of these interviews were conducted in English. Several, however, were conducted in Hebrew. Issuing from either situation, as well as for reason of common courtesy, I afforded the respondents an opportunity to read the text of his or her conversation and to emend their remarks. Most of the writers made extremely frugal use of this opportunity. A few made more extensive emendations than I would have preferred.

In only one instance was the conversation so much "improved" that I dropped it from the book.

Yet a different language problem is that of conveying both Hebrew and Yiddish terms that if translated directly into English in the conversational text would ring false. What I have done instead has been to gloss these terms (or provide what seems to me vital information on passing events or persons) at their first appearance in brackets. For example, because even among native English-speakers the word "immigrants" is almost never employed, *olim* (see above) is retained and glossed in place. Wherever it appears thereafter, no special explanation is provided.

Where to draw that line? Hardly an exacting business, "Shabbat" is not glossed; nor are "kibbutz," and "Hanukkah." However, "Shavuot" is identified as [Pentecost]. Dates are provided for "I. L. Peretz" but not for "Maimonides," identification for "Ras Burka incident" but not "Talmud." I fully recognize that glosses for terms like *Hasid* [Jewish pietists] and *Palmach* generation [the Forties] are grossly inadequate as full-bodied explanations, but they do sufficiently serve, I think, the purpose at hand. However, for more than the usual author's motives, I would strongly suggest that readers not abreast of the Israeli or Jewish scene read the interviews in sequence.

When the sum of conversations reached a total of 18 [*chai*, symbolic Hebrew number signifying "life"], it felt appropriate to come to a halt.

In retrospect, Israeli writers seem to me notably hospitable and remarkably patient with all the incumbrances of "getting interviewed." I just might add that if at times Interlocutor HC exasperates through over-politeness, density, or ineptitude at exploiting Respondent's waverings or inconsistencies, let me confess that he sometimes drives me to distraction as well. No one can be more exquisitely sensitive than I to leads permitted to slip or lines of inquiry which should have been either sooner dropped or more energetically pursued. I can only admire the demeanor of this procession of Israeli writers who suffered my lapses with such good grace.

Aside from the many of these encounters that first appeared in the pages of the *Jewish Frontier*, the others, in whole or part, were first published in *Manasseh*, *Reform Judaism*, *Moment*, and *Ariel*. Following their own constraints of space or policy, sometimes these publications abridged or otherwise edited the original text. I have taken this opportunity to restore those original portions.

Acknowledgments

My special thanks to Mitchell Cohen and Mordecai Newman
for helping me to keep my eye on the quarry; to Bernice
and Paul Stone for their kind help at a stage of this project;
and most particularly to my wife, Marcia, for her support,
editorial expertise, and immense patience.

Aharon Appelfeld

Not to the Left, Not to the Right

I knew him through two stunning novels, Badenheim 1939 *and*
The Age of Wonders, *the latter of which I had written about in*
laudatory fashion in The Jerusalem Post. *Appelfeld recalled the*
review, and we arranged to meet on a November afternoon in 1983
at the Atara, a generally crowded café in downtown Jerusalem.

"Don't worry," he added reassuringly. "I haven't much hair on
my head. We'll find each other." When I arrived, a heavy-domed,
broad-shouldered figure in a red-checked shirt approached me
from an inside corner table. It was he, an Atara regular. He took
me courteously in tow, and from the start assumed the role of host.

It was immediately plain that Appelfeld preferred conversation
to an interview. He evinced surprising interest in my background,
interests, and activities. He is both an attentive listener and a pre-
cise speaker. His accent in English, not one of the several lan-
guages for which he makes claim, bears the indeterminate cast of
Mittel-Europa. It serves him more than adequately; in the course
of several hours, only two or three times did he have cause to
reach for a more exact term. He leaned close over the table, in an
attitude of friendly intimacy. His eyes are particularly lively,
and, to be sure, he is far from hirsute. In the course of 1½ hours,
four times he popped up from his seat, once to collar the retiring
waitress so that she would take our order, other times to greet ac-
quaintances at nearby tables. Much in his element, Appelfeld at
his corner table at the Atara seemed in his second home.

Haim Chertok: What do you best recall of your early years in
Europe, the scene of your fiction or, at least, all of your fiction
that's been translated?

Aharon Appelfeld: I was born in Czernowitz, in Bukovina, into
an assimilated Jewish home. It was then in Rumania, but later
became a part of the Ukraine.

HC: Just like my grandmother's native city of Drogobycz. She
spoke Polish, but the city was then included in the Austrian
Empire.

AA: Drogobycz, you know, is the city of Bruno Schulz [1892–1942], a really remarkable writer. He was the first translator of Kafka into Polish.

HC: Yes, not long ago I read Schulz's *Sanatorium Under the Sign of the Hourglass.* It's extraordinary. What language did you speak at home?

AA: We spoke German. That was typical of assimilated Jewish households. I was eight-and-a-half when the war came. My mother was killed, and I was sent to a labor camp in the Ukraine. From there I escaped and lived for three years in the woods. Fortunately, my face was not particularly Jewish in appearance. Then for three years I worked for a Soviet army unit. In 1946—I was then thirteen—I was transported to this country along with many other unattached youngsters. Brought here by the authorities, we just came.

HC: So you did not have any formal primary education?

AA: That's right. In fact, in all my life I have never attended regular school. I arrived in Palestine with no luggage, no family, no education—nothing. For the first three years, I worked on a farm near Jerusalem.

HC: A private farm?

AA: No, there was a group of us. It was part of a planned program. We worked six hours a day and spent two hours learning Hebrew. After that, for the following two-and-a-half years I was mobilized into the army.

HC: So all the trepidation about going to school and final examinations in *The Age of Wonders* is totally imagined.

AA: Yes, of course. That's how I imagined it would be.

HC: And after the army?

AA: I entered Hebrew University in Jerusalem. My subject was Yiddish literature. Now I can read many languages, but then Yiddish was for me a special vehicle into my past and myself, which is why I consciously chose to study it. But more, study alone can be superficial, so I chose to live in the religious quarter of Jerusalem—in Mea Shearim. I studied Yiddish and the Bible and surrounded myself with Jews who did not hate themselves. Because I had lived through so many years of personal and cultural disorientation, I pursued my Yiddish studies at the university for eight years! This included a period of deep crisis for me, "dark days" you might call them. I had repressed much that I had experienced and felt from the Holocaust years. And it was not I alone.

You must understand the period of the late Forties and Fifties. *There* stood those confident Israelis and *here* were we recent arrivals from Europe. Between the newcomers and the *real* Israelis there yawned an ideological chasm. Indoctrination was constant and heavy-handed. The Israeli—a sort of blond type— was a new Jew; the Holocaust was just a bad word. It implied shame, of lambs being led to slaughter. Of course, today we know much more, but though now we come close to dwelling on the Holocaust, *then* it was not spoken of. It was as if we victims were being silently accused, and we all shared a deep sense of embarrassment.

The cultural climate did not change until the Eichmann trial. Only then did the subject of the Holocaust emerge as discussible, as something legitimate to talk about.

HC: Would you currently describe yourself as a religious Jew?

AA: When I arrived in this country at the age of thirteen, the religious community was very small. Anyone who reads *The Retreat* or *The Age of Wonders* can easily tell that I was raised in an assimilated home. But the cauldron of the Holocaust has drawn me very close to the Jewish people. My three years in the camps were fundamental to my self-understanding. I may not wear a *kippa* [skullcap], but I am a religious Jew.

HC: I am curious: do or did you send your own children to religious schools?

AA: My wife and I have three children: two sons who will shortly be serving in the army and a younger child. One son, by the way, is a gifted violinist. And if you could see the walls in our home in Mevasseret Zion [suburb ten kilometers west of Jerusalem], you would see on display some sketches and drawings which are the work of my other talented son. For their primary education, my children attended state religious schools. All three share my own warm attitude toward Jewish tradition and are, each in his own way, "religious."

The Oriental [Sephardic] Jews, you see, come by their Jewishness, their heritage, more naturally than do we former Europeans. Their religious shell is not yet crystallized; their background is their culture. But Labor Zionism was for so long a specifically anti-religious, secular rebellion *against* Judaism that for many of us, religion must be reclaimed. The oddity now is that Zionism is increasingly becoming a religious movement.

HC: Your children, then, have not rebelled against your values or outlook?

AA: On the contrary, they share my approach of openness and dialogue with all Jewish people. As I hope is clear from my novels, it is important to comprehend all Jews as human beings and to recognize that secular Jews are, of course, Jews.

There are two falsifying tendencies toward Judaism to which we are heir: first, the nostalgic, sentimental approach of those who tried to sweeten Judaism, exemplified best in the works of I. L. Peretz [1851–1915]. Then there were the ideologues like Mendele Mocher Seforim [1836–1918] and Joseph Hayyim Brenner [1881–1921], the anti-religious social critics. We live today in the space between those two approaches. At present, the critical element is on the defensive; the nostalgic seems to be prevailing. Both, however, are superficial. As I tried to demonstrate in *The Age of Wonders*, life is nothing if not complicated. Each person contains endless contradictions.

HC: So you consider yourself a religious writer?

AA: Of course. Our religion is the pre-eminent expression of Jewishness, the essence of our culture. To me, Jewish culture without a religious basis is unimaginable. But I don't mean to talk narrowly about this. The core of our culture, which is the insistence that life has a moral purpose, may be found among the so-called secular as well. The Labor Zionism of the *kibbutznikim* has emitted authentic Jewishness. Especially in our earlier years there were many people for whom the Hebrew language itself was a religious vehicle. Reclaiming it from the past and from exclusively religious matters constituted a genuine religious experience for them. In reality, even communism is a distorted form of Jewish messianism.

HC: Do you think the present tilt toward messianism in Israeli life poses any serious dangers?

AA: Authentic messianism is a permanent legacy of Judaism. The *Hasidim* [Jewish pietists] have internalized their messianism. When they pray, the leave behind "the Egypt of the heart" and strive for a vision of perfection, a purification of their impulses.

HC: And in its political manifestations?

AA: Political messianism is a cheapening of the impulse. We sometimes forget that we are living not very long after a period of almost unparalleled catastrophe. It is a time both of danger and of transition. Messianism is one of many competing tendencies today. There are many people who live in Israel who are not fully at home here. They live in a *galut* [exile] of the heart. For them in particular, messianism has its attractions.

HC: Let me turn, at last, to your writing. You've published seventeen works of fiction of which three [now five] have appeared in English. When did you begin?

AA: Well, all the while I was studying Yiddish I was, of course, also studying Hebrew language and literature, for although Hebrew was not my language, I knew I had to come to terms with it. As I have mentioned, I was very conscious of the need to confront my past, to investigate through language and literature what it means to be a Jew. I started to write in order to make discoveries about myself. That is still the case. And I'll tell you the truth: writing saved me!

HC: From what?

AA [smiling]: Just that. It saved me. You know that the assimilated Jews of Central Europe had tried to escape from themselves—just like Otto Weiniger [Austrian psychologist, 1880–1903] in *Nefesh Yehudi* [*The Soul of the Jew,* by Yehoshua Sobel], the play Israel sent recently to the Edinburgh Festival. The self-hatred was too typical.

HC: Yes, but when did you actually begin to write?

AA: Why I was writing all the while, but my education had its black holes, and I wasn't confident of Hebrew as an instrument. So at first I wrote a lot of sentimental poetry. Feelings were expressed, but the poems were burdened with the cultural baggage that I took from my reading—from books. It took a long time for my writing to reach a level of integrity, to be any good. My first book was not published until I reached the age of thirty.

HC: Then you began to teach, am I right?

AA: Yes, I began my teaching in night schools, then went on to teacher seminaries and such. For some years now I have been teaching Hebrew literature [and recently Holocaust Studies] at Ben-Gurion University in Beersheba. Although sometimes, naturally, the grading of papers interferes with my writing schedule, I enjoy the teaching. There is no serious conflict.

HC: Has your recent fame affected your professional life as a teacher?

AA: No, not at all.

HC: What is your major goal in presenting Holocaust material to college-aged Israelis?

AA: My aim is to impart an attitude, an atmosphere to the students. To create an environment wherein one can speak freely about the Holocaust, to free oneself from inhibitions. The problems are great because the Holocaust has been abused and misused, and the slate must be wiped clean before one can begin. A language to deal with the immensity of the event must be found or created—one neither too emotional nor too rational.

For a long while, the victims have wanted just to forget what happened to them. And the others have been content not to hear: they are afraid of it. It's a sort of quiet conspiracy. Even more than among the Americans I used to teach at Hebrew Union College in Jerusalem, this condition is prevalent among Israeli students. We have a long Zionist tradition against the Diaspora as *galut*. There was also the belief that Zionist theory justified itself with the Holocaust, proving that Diaspora Jews were defenseless and therefore destined for disaster. It is, of course, a cruel, unpleasant argument—even sinful. It implies an accusation or guilt against the victims, and Zionism seemed a ready weapon to turn against the survivors. It was very painful.

HC: Which writers do you admire? Which have you emulated or learned from?

AA: The Bible is very important to me, not only as an ancient source of inspiration but even stylistically: the adjectives are minimal and emotion gets presented instead of analyzed. I learned a great deal about how to use the Hebrew language as a modern tool from Joseph Hayyim Brenner and S. Y. Agnon [1888–1970]. Then there are the great European Jewish writers—Kafka and Proust, for example. Their fiction is transparently the work of assimilated Jews—hypersensitive. That's very Jewish, I think. And even Joyce picked a Jew as the hero of his era. I know the American writers—Bellow, Malamud, Roth—but as the critics correctly say, I am closer to Kafka. Then there are some Jewish writers who are so assimilated that they cannot really be counted as Jews at all.

HC: Have you ever, like Bruno, the survivor in *The Age of Wonders*, returned to visit Europe?

AA [abruptly]: No! Only to England. I have no interest in returning myself.

HC: In the final section of that novel, why did you send Bruno back?

AA: It is, I think, important because of the danger of selectively sweet memories of the past, or nostalgia dominating the tone. But things really have not changed in Austria. In fact, Bruno is not really all that different from his father.

HC: But he always takes care to identify himself as a Jew, or rather, as a resident of Jerusalem.

AA: No, he reacts only when they ask him. He merely reacts.

HC: Speaking of assimilation, you recently spent a year teaching and lecturing in the United States. How did you enjoy it?

AA: That isn't an easy thing for me to talk about. I met many wonderful people, and yes, my books are well-received there. The next one, by the one way, *The Retreat,* is with a new publisher—Dutton. My first American publisher [Godine] was very nice, but distribution was limited. How did you find the translations?

HC: Really excellent.

AA: Good. I have kept the same translator [Dalya Bilu]. I also think that she is very good. [His latest translator is Jeffrey M. Green.] But I am avoiding your question. America is a very sad place. To tell you the truth, it made me ill and sad. I don't want to hurt anyone; I met so many sensitive, intelligent, genuinely nice people in my year of teaching at Harvard and Brandeis. Nearly half the professors there are Jews. Nice, lovely people living where Jewish life has no future. And then I met the professional Jews, absurd ones making absurd claims like "there's more hope for Jews in America than in Israel," or insisting on the positive benefits for Judaism in intermarriage. They are amazing!

HC: Then I take it that you are glad to be back here in front of a bowl of soup in a café in Jerusalem.

AA: Without question! Of course I'm happy to be sitting with you here in Jerusalem or content at my desk in Mevasseret Zion. I must tell you, people thought we were crazy when we first moved out there, especially since I don't drive. And ten years ago it was just a pile of rocks. But my work has gone well there, and we love it. As you know as well as I, Israel is a land in constant turmoil, a place with too much vulgarity, even at times of brutality. But this is also a place of enormous vitality. Yes, I am fully at home here.

HC: You mean that America bears resemblance to the world of *Badenheim 1939?*

AA: Just so! You see, the spiritual Holocaust has already happened in America. Of course you can't go around just telling people that, but there it is! It's the truth. For the Jew, America is a spiritual Holocaust.

HC: Are you conscious of the Holocaust's being exploited?

AA: Unfortunately, yes. It has been vulgarized, over-used, and commercialized. It's a sellable product, and it is used by both Jews and non-Jews.

HC: Israeli writers are frequently known to take positions on public issues. You seem successfully to avoid doing that.

AA [smiling]: Very true. I tell you, my political orientation is Jewish. Not to the left, not to the right. Simply "Jewish." I do differ from many of my fellow writers. They respect my withdrawal from political activity. But you also should be aware that my background, like that of nearly all of my fellow writers, is the Labor Party. It was the carrier of the dominant milieu, a cultural movement embodying both the socialist and the Jewish traditions. Labor really was what Zionism was all about.

Today it is quite different, and there is a deep crisis among the intelligentsia in the country. Who are we? Jews? Westerners? Of the Middle East? We have no serviceable models, few answers. When I first came to this country, there *were* models, an elite people who lived out the ideals of Zionism. We have lost this world, this elite from the Forties and Fifties. Today we are unquestionably a confused country. There is a heightening of vulgarity. There is an absence of leadership. Modesty seems lost. There are Jews who belong to movements receiving enormous publicity that teach that those who disagree with them are not really Jews at all! It reminds me of the time when the Temple was destroyed. There was no prophecy: only idiots were found in the land. So we have lost our orientation, and this affects the intelligentsia as much as, if not more than, others. For these reasons, therefore, I try to keep my politics "Jewish."

HC: Do you ascribe any religious significance to the fact or existence of the State of Israel itself?

AA: No, the state is only a frame within which to live. For the Jewish people it is, of course, a wonderful and vital thing—but still no more than a frame. Further, despite what I said before, I recognize that it is not a suitable frame for all Jews.

Gabriel Preil, that extraordinarily fine Hebrew poet, lives in a small, dark, depressing apartment in the Bronx. He is now in his seventies, and he is the last of a small group of Hebrew-language poets in New York. Some years ago a group of us arranged for him a modest fund and an apartment in which to live in bright, sunny Israel. As you might easily imagine, he hadn't made much money writing Hebrew poetry in New York, so he came. Here in Israel he lived among friends and admirers in a climate that seemed in every conceivable way more agreeable. And yet he could not function. After a time, Preil returned to his gloomy Bronx apartment.

HC: Do you associate closely with other Israeli writers?

AA: Of course. I know them all. We all know each other. Natan Zach is my neighbor. Carmi was sitting at that table [pointing behind me] just ten minutes ago. I taught at the same place as Yehuda Amichai. We are all close.

HC: Isn't it strange that after forty years in the country, you still don't write about Israeli life?

AA: I suppose so, but there it is! I ask myself what to write about Israel, and I don't know. Here the pot is still boiling, but what do I know about the intimate side of the lives of Moroccans? Nothing. Eastern Europe can be dealt with. I don't, however, feel as though I'm writing only about the past. Although I was only eight years old, for me it's not, after all, just memory. For me it's *now*, and in it I try to capture the core, the essence of Jewish life and character. Time and place are really just a matter of convenience, not of the essence.

In one way I am, I think, unique among the Hebrew writers: my closest friends, the ones who came with me from Europe, can't read my work in Hebrew. I write for them, but they can't read me.

HC: The critics who do read you, in English anyway, have been universally appreciative. That, at least, must be very gratifying.

AA: Yes, but it is not entirely the case. Have you seen the article by Ruth Wisse in last August's *Commentary*? She said some really terrible things: that my writing is filled with self-hatred and hatred of Jews. I couldn't believe it when I read it. She writes that I condemn the victims. The *victims*! A vicious article! Read it when you can.

Later I did locate that Commentary *article on Appelfeld by Ruth Wisse. The novelist's reaction seemed sufficiently justified to move me to write an article which aimed to answer and qualify her contention. Entitled "Appelfeld and Affirmation," it appeared in the Jerusalem-published cultural quarterly* Ariel *(No. 61) in 1985.*

T. Carmi

To Heal the Breach

In May of 1984 a friend, Rabbi Ben Hollander, helped to arrange a meeting between me and his colleague at Jerusalem's Hebrew Union College, poet T. Carmi. The weather was balmy when I arrived at the handsome, recessed building next to the stately King David Hotel. Classes had ended for the semester; students, nearly all American, had fled. Talking on the phone when I entered his office, Carmi was seated behind a desk that seemed, in comparison to my own, very orderly. He is a well-knit man in his late 50s. His face is furrowed; his voice expressive, resonant.

Carmi is the recipient of most of Israel's major literary awards: the Shlonsky Prize for Poetry, the Brenner Prize for Literature, the Prime Minister's Prize for Creative Writing. He was born in New York City in 1925 and grew up in a Hebrew-speaking household. Emigrating to Israel in 1947, Carmi fought in the War of Independence. Among his many volumes of poetry, four, including the dual-language publication of At the Stone of Losses, *have appeared in English-language editions. In 1981 he completed translating and editing* The Penguin Book of Hebrew Verse, *a book whose appearance was hailed by critic Harold Bloom in these terms: "This admirable anthology has no rivals in Hebrew or English"* (New York Review of Books). *An adept translator, Carmi has brought Sophocles, Shakespeare, Giraudoux, and Brecht, among others, into Hebrew.*

Haim Chertok [passing Carmi a periodical]: You know, you were unwittingly present one day last fall when I was talking with Aharon Appelfeld at the Café Atara. I mentioned it, in fact, in the published interview here in the *Jewish Frontier* [March 1984]. Appelfeld's point was that the circle of Israeli artists and writers is relatively small and that you encounter one another all the time.

T. Carmi: He's absolutely right. I do remember seeing him talking one day to someone—yourself, it seems—that day at the Atara. But it's too nice a day to languish indoors. Shall we go to a café ourselves?

HC: By all means.

TC [after driving to the nearby, outdoor Café of the Park and then ordering coffee, Carmi nods a greeting to a white-haired man seated at a nearby table]: Here now is another instance of Appelfeld's notion. Just behind you to the left is Ben-Zion Orgad, the well-known composer. We were introduced just last week at a concert where a poem of mine was set to music by Noah Guy. Now here we see each other again.

HC: I understand that your eleventh volume of poetry has recently been published. Ben Hollander mentioned a public reading.

TC: Yes. *At The Stone of Losses* is a joint publication of the University of California at Berkeley and the Jewish Publication Society as part of its Jewish Poetry project, a very worthwhile series of publications.

HC: Yes, I agree with you. Not long ago I reviewed Moyshe-Leyb Halpern's [1886–1932] collection *In New York* in that JPS poetry series for the [*Jerusalem*] *Post.* It's a fascinating sequence of poems. Some of *In New York* reminded me of Lorca's *A Poet in New York.*

TC [Pause]: My public reading at the Van Leer Institute went very well. By the way, have you heard that my translator, Grace Schulman, has just won the Kenneth B. Smilen *Present Tense* Award for Hebrew–English translation?

HC [Smiling]: No. That's one prize I have never heard about . . . but I'm sure she is deserving. Still, I am a trifle perplexed. You grew up in the States, and obviously your English is flawless, perfectly natural. Why have you always used translators?

TC: It's very simple: I am neither an English poet, nor is English my language for writing. English is my native tongue, but to write *poetry* in English feels alien.

HC: Well, that seems to answer why you don't write poetry in English. But I asked something else. You are, after all, a professional and highly talented translator. Not to translate your own work seems almost perverse.

TC: I always collaborate with my translators. That is important. And with each translation—this one is my fourth—the translator has sought *me* out rather than the other way around. That also seems important to me. But I don't think employing a translator perverse under the circumstances. I can't think of many writers who are equally effective in several languages.

HC: Nabokov. Joseph Brodsky . . .

TC: He's now writing in English? Yes, I suppose that he is.

HC: A while back I reviewed Natan Zach's recent collection— *The Static Element*—when it appeared in English. It did not come off very well. In the end I wasn't sure where to pin the blame: on the poet or on the translator.

TC: Peter Everwine, the American poet, did the translation. There is a real problem with Zach's poetry. It's hard to render the charged flatness of the original, the playfulness with the colloquial diction.

HC: It's just the opposite with Amichai's poetry. He translates without apparent loss or effort. Tell me, how professionally significant is it for an Israeli poet to be translated and published internationally?

TC: The important thing is that the translation is a test. Faults tend to get magnified. Every word, every line gets reappraised. In fact, while working on a translation, occasionally we may make changes in the original text of the poems themselves. The second thing, of course, is that it is exciting to reach a wider circle of readers, to get reactions from strangers. That's part of the fun.

HC: In the body of your poetry, which now covers a period of nearly forty years, the pain of war seems to be a central preoccupation.

TC: Really?

HC: You think not? I was thinking of longer poems like "Military Funeral at High Noon" and "Author's Apology." I have not only enjoyed them but have taught them, in fact, to my English-language students at WUJS [World Union of Jewish Students]

Institute in Arad where I teach Israeli literature. We have something in common there, it seems: we both teach American
students in Israel. In any event, your poems score a significant
impact.

TC: Now that I think about it, I suppose that you have a point,
though actually I think of myself as more of a lyrical poet, more
personal than public in my themes. When I spoke at a workshop
at the Van Leer Institute not long ago, I found it fascinating but
very difficult to explain to others how I organize my material
structurally. One obvious shift is that the earlier poems are those
of a combatant, the more recent those of an aging reservist. In
"Another View" I was trying to depict the two levels of con-
sciousness—subterranean and surface—that Israelis exhibited
after the Six Day War. Later I attempted something similar in
"Author's Apology," but by then the cellar had flooded the rest of
the house. The two levels had become intertwined.

But you know, I suspect that the same technique and theme—
the interfusion of the inner voice and the outer—crop up in the
love poems as well.

HC: You fought in the War of Independence, didn't you?

TC: Yes, I came here in 1947 at the age of twenty-two. My father
is Bernard Charny, an Orthodox rabbi and educator. He and my
brother made *aliya* [emigration to Israel] after I came. My brother
is now a clinical psychologist at Tel Aviv University. He was the
organizer of the recently held Israel Genocide Conference.

HC: You, Yehuda Amichai, Amir Gilboa, the others who fought
in 1948 are inevitably viewed as members of a particular, very
special generation. How do you perceive the difference in sen-
sibility, in outlook, or even in technique between yourselves and
the generation of poets now in their thirties and forties, most of
whom seem to be based in Tel Aviv rather than Jerusalem?

TC: I don't usually think in terms of poetic generations.

HC: Let me put it this way. In general, both my WUJS students
and I are more responsive to your poems and those of your peers

than to the typical poetry of younger Israeli poets like Yair Hurvitz and Yona Wallach. It is not merely that your poems are
more accessible. We *like* them. Would you conjecture why this
might be the case?

TC: Well, let me try. In general, the younger poets you're talking about tend on principle to be anti-ideological and extremely
individualistic. Their poems emphasize textural elements often
at the expense of organic structure. There is a dearth of metaphorical development and more a barrage of discrete sensual
impressions.

But you know, many of these tendencies can be perceived in
the early work of Amir Gilboa. He first made his mark as "an
experimental poet." So it is not really new with any generation.
The crucial break, however, occurred in the late 1950s when
Anglo-American poetry became the dominant influence here.
John Ashberry has recently been translated into Hebrew. As you
are probably aware, there are critics who claim it's an error to try
to understand Ashberry.

HC: I find that hard to fathom. Returning to the Israeli literary
scene, much contemporary Hebrew verse seems to look elsewhere for its inspiration: the Incas, Tibet, you-name-it. Everywhere but to Jewish sources.

TC: There is no doubt that traditional Hebrew sources are simply
not available to many younger poets. The result is a loss of resonance, an absence of tension between the new and the old, the
sacred and the profane. Street Hebrew itself has become something of an ideology.

HC: Which of the younger poets do you enjoy reading?

TC: Oh, I like Meir Wieseltier. Also Rami Ditsani and [Avraham] Balaban.

HC: In his latest book, Philip Larkin describes how he prepared
the newest edition of the *Oxford Anthology of Twentieth-Century
Poetry.* Apparently, after reading all the other anthologies, for
six months he made the basement of the Bodleian Library his

hermitage. He read every conceivably interesting poet's complete works straight through! How did you . . .?

TC [Nodding]: . . . Yes, it was something very much like that, but it took me five years of camping out at the Schocken Institute. I tracked down books that were long out of print, scholarly publications, *mahzorim* [holiday prayerbooks]. Locating the texts for the *Penguin Anthology* was an extended voyage of discovery. I hadn't any idea how ignorant I was. And after that it took me seven years more of editorial work to finish the job.

HC: Twelve years! Well, you have the satisfaction of knowing that it has completely swept the field, superseding all its predecessors. When you first started, how long did you anticipate it would take to complete the job?

TC: Perhaps three years. But I'm giving a false impression if you think it was onerous. On the contrary, there was the tremendous excitement of dealing with almost forgotten materials. Even now there remains a large body of unpublished works. Ezra Fleisher has just published 200 substantial poems from the *Geniza* [storage area in a synagogue containing worn and discarded religious materials which are not destroyed because they contain the name of God] of Cairo [the most famous such repository, dating from 882].

HC: In his otherwise adulatory review of the *Penguin Book of Hebrew Verse*, Harold Bloom refers to James Kugel's attack on your initial premise that a tradition of Hebrew poetry may be said to exist in the first place. Bloom himself seems persuaded of a discontinuity in the tradition too profound to enable you justifiably, in any meaningful sense, to use the concept. After all, if the Jews of the biblical period understood no real notion of poetry as distinct from prose, or rather non-poetry, what sort of tradition can be spoken of?

TC: I am familiar with Kugel's argument, and I found his book [*The Idea of Biblical Poetry*] fascinating.

HC: I agree with you. I spoke with him last year when he was here in Jerusalem on sabbatical.

TC: Some of what he discusses is too technical to go into now, but what it comes down to, I think, is very much an instance of the glass being half filled or half empty. Take the famous poet and mathematician Abraham Ibn Ezra who in the twelfth century wrote a furious critique of the seventh-century *paytan* [maker of pious verses, Eleazer] Kallir. Ibn Ezra traveled throughout Europe—Italy, Germany, England—systematically converting Hebrew poets to the Andalusian (Spanish) School of poetry. This is a marvelous instance of the continuity of tradition in Hebrew poetry that Kugel relegates to a passing footnote. Wherever and whenever there have been lapses of cultural amnesia, there and then there have been Jewish poets who have spontaneously attempted to heal the breach.

HC: Like, say, Carmi?

TC [Ignoring my comment]: So basically I differ with both Kugel and Bloom. Dialogue over the centuries—the *piyut* [pious poetry] with the Bible, Ibn Ezra with Kallir, [Hayim Nachman] Bialik [1873–1934] with [Solomon] Ibn Gabirol [11th century, Spain], [Nathan] Alterman [1910–1970] with Immanuel of Rome [9th century]—has everything to do with the nature of literary continuity.

HC: Not long ago, Amos Oz concluded his tour of Israel's horizon, *In the Land of Israel,* by commenting that our present morale and moral condition "is not good." In the light of the recent arrests of members of a network of Jewish terrorists on the West Bank and this very week's disclosure that after the Ashkelon bus hijacking, the two Arab surviving terrorists were clubbed to death by members of the security forces, Oz's verdict may sound to some like understatement. Unlike Oz, you chose to come on *aliya* as a young man of twenty-two. Do you occasionally look back with the feeling that something has gone fundamentally wrong here?

TC: What we are witnessing is the brutalization of Israeli society that people like Meron Benvenisti [editor of *West Bank Data Project*] predicted would occur because of the occupation of the

territories. A significant number of Jews has succumbed to
pseudo-messianism. The result is Jewish terrorism and tacit
support for brutality by people who see their foes as anonymous,
who arc in fact incapable of really seeing them at all.

HC: It *is* a fearful development. Just yesterday evening my
daughter Jennifer, who is now doing national service with *Sherut
Leumi* [public service option for religiously observant young
women, in lieu of military training], was arguing that Arab terrorists should be killed and that neither she nor her friends
cared how. My wife and I felt she had taken steps down a path
away from human values we think inviolable.

TC: The point must be made clearly: you just don't kill captives.
Of course in every war, including 1948, there have been isolated
acts of inhumanity, but the difference now is that a major current of public opinion tries to vindicate them. It's the pseudo-
messianism that makes the difference. Imagine a minister in the
government [Yuval Ne'eman, Minister of Science and Develop-
ment] making a learned distinction between murdering bus pas-
sengers and murdering mayors! It's Dr. Strangelove.

HC: Especially here in Israel, truth seems to pale fiction. In a
different area—the theater—censorship has recently figured as
public issue. It seems to happen here periodically. Novelist
Aharon Megged has been particularly forceful in denouncing it.
In addition to being a poet and teacher, as an accomplished
translator of classic and modern dramatists, you are also known
as a man of the theater. Do you find censorship to be a serious
problem or personally burdensome?

TC: The first thing to be said is that censorship is usually good
for box office. It's the best publicity imaginable. I personally
have never experienced any problems. The real difficulties lie in
the Arab sector. There the problem of censorship is very serious.

HC: Do you have any friends among the Arab writers?

TC: No.

HC: How long have you been teaching literature at Hebrew
Union College?

TC: Five years now. The students are good, *very* good. Their year in Jerusalem is their first year of rabbinical study, and they are all dedicated, perhaps over-dedicated, to doing well.

HC: Do many make *aliya?*

TC: Very few. I can think of only two or three. After all, they all plan careers as Reform rabbis. [Glancing at his watch,] May I drive you anyplace?

HC: Yes, in fact—the Central Bus Station.

TC [driving through the city]: Such heavy traffic is very unusual for this time of day.

HC: It probably has something to do with *Yom Yerushalayim* [Jerusalem Day] festivities. My daughter and her friends are now en route here. They plan to dance much of the night away at the *kotel* [Western Wall of the Temple].

TC: Is it really *Yom Yerushalayim?* I wasn't aware.

HC: Hunh! How could you possibly have missed it? You may be out of the basement of the Schocken Institute, but you must be deeply involved in something else.

TC: Well . . . yes. I am supposed to be starting on a translation of *Cyrano.* The Haifa Theater is currently playing my translation of *Much Ado About Nothing,* and the Chamber Theater will produce my *Measure for Measure* sometime next season. Also, Beersheba's theater company is planning to do my *Midsummer Night's Dream.* Translating Shakespeare into Hebrew, now *that's* hard work!

HC: But for you, at least, not as hard as translating Carmi into English! Oh, I nearly forgot, what *does* the mysterious T. stand for, anyway?

TC: Oh, Carmi is actually my first name. My full name is Carmi Charny. I'm often called things like Tuvia or Teddy, but T. Carmi is how it has worked out. My friends just call me Carmi.

HC: Wasn't it strange growing up in New York as a Hebrew-speaker? This was before there were so many Queens *yordim* [emigrants from Israel].

TC: Not at all. Especially since we had lived in Palestine between the years I was six and eight. Hebrew has always been perfectly natural for me.

HC: You mentioned that your father was a rabbi. Did you abandon traditional religious observances after you arrived in Israel? Religious imagery does not seem to play a major role in your work the way that it does in Amichai's, for example.

TC: No, I gave up ritualized Judaism. But you know, it would not surprise me to learn that I actually employed *more* religious material or allusions than does Amichai.

HC: Perhaps, but unlike Amichi, your own doubts play no real thematic role in your poetry, not, at least, that I can detect.

TC: I suppose that you're right. I've never really thought much about it. [Arriving at the bus station,] Here we are. You can cross right here.

HC: Thank you very much. I hope to catch your *Midsummer Night's Dream* when it plays in Beersheba.

TC: It was a pleasure.

Only later, on the bus ride back to Yeroham, did I realize that I still had not learned the source or meaning of that enigmatic capital T.

A. B. Yehoshua

Dismantler

*Close to noon on a day in September 1984, less than a week after
Shimon Peres and Yitzhak Shamir had reached their accord to
form a government of "National Unity," I caught the 5:30 A.M.
bus out of Yeroham for the 5-hour ride from the Negev to Haifa to
meet with novelist A. B. Yehoshua at his home. Five of his books
have appeared in English, most notably* The Lover *(1978) and*
A Late Divorce *(1984). A native of Israel, Yehoshua is one of the
younger Israeli writers who have established an international
reputation. His accommodationist position toward Palestinian
national aims, his revisionism of Zionism, and his critical stance
toward the Diaspora as set out in his polemic* Between Right and
Right *(1981) have met with considerable attention. I had not met
him previously.*

*Two Yeroham friends grew excited when I informed them of
my prospective encounter. Chaim Goldberg called Yehoshua "a
philosophical Canaanite" who was "just plain inaccurate about*
yerida [*Jewish emigration from Israel*] *and about Jewishness.
Push him on this!" Roni Brown, on the other hand, was visibly
envious. "He's not only the first Israeli novelist I read all the way
through in Hebrew. He is also the very best. Let him know. I wish I
were going." I had, then, both my own agenda and a hometown
mandate.*

*Arriving some 30 minutes late at a house that hugs a Haifa
hillside, I was hailed from below by someone on the steps. It was
a friendly voice, and soon I was ushered into a large, tidy apartment. His head rimmed by a mane of unruly, wavy hair, Yehoshua—born in 1936—looks younger than his years. A cordial
host, he is also extremely voluble. He introduced me to his teen-
aged daughter on her way out of the apartment, then led me into
a small, orderly study that contained a sofa and a crowded book-
case. We sat by a large desk.*

Haim Chertok: I'm sorry that I'm late. What with two changes of
buses, it's difficult to estimate exactly how long the trip from

Yeroham should take. It took longer, in fact, than it used to take me to fly from California to New York.

A. B. Yehoshua: Think nothing of it. I think it's a remarkable thing for you to choose to live in a development area. In today's Israel, you are a pioneer of pioneers. Really, one among our modern saints. To come from California to live in Yeroham. Imagine!

HC: I don't feel like a living martyr. I know that for an Israeli, the gap between Haifa and Yeroham seems enormous, but coming from America, one's perspective changes. I find no essential difference, and Yeroham possesses certain advantages that are important to me. It's been no great sacrifice.

ABY: Anyway, you don't have to martyr your appetite. Let me get you some refreshments. [With Yehoshua out of the room, I noticed that most of the books on the shelves appeared to deal with psychology. He returned shortly with cold drinks and a tray of cookies.] And from California you came!

HC [Motioning to the bookshelves]: Thank you. You seem to have a strong interest in psychology.

ABY: Oh, this is my wife's office. She's a psychoanalyst. [We drink.] Only here in Israel can a Jew experience being a full person, don't you agree? In the Diaspora, Jews are never truly free fully to be themselves because they are forever defining themselves against other Jews: either associating with or separating themselves from the larger Jewish community. In Israel alone can Jews achieve normalcy. Only here can they freely act, can they *be* free. Only here is total Judaism.

HC: "Total Judaism"? I'm not sure what you mean. Aren't there enclaves of "total Judaism" in Brooklyn, in Los Angeles, and in Antwerp?

ABY: No! No! What sort of freedom can you find in an enclave? I am talking about a Jewish environment that is as natural for Jews as France is for the French. That is to say, in *all* the aspects of life—economics, politics, communications—every-

thing is Jewish. America can never provide that for its Jews.
Jews in the Diaspora fear the total Judaism which *is* Israel. *Aliya* is the only logical alternative for Jews who want to be free.
The aim of Zionism was to create the very ground of our freedom, to create a space where we aren't doomed to have to walk
around forever questioning what our Jewishness is. Here it simply
is, like the Frenchness of a Frenchman.

HC: But don't we seem to debate the Jewishness of the Jew—the
perpetual "Who is a Jew?"—here more fiercely than ever? It
has seemed to me that the inner logic of assuming what you call
the "fullness of Judaism" entails not only *aliya* but some kind of
religious involvement or commitment.

ABY: Not necessarily. Total Judaism need not be religious. I myself do come from a religious background. Still, though religious
culture is part of my very language, Judaism is for me not the
Jewish religion but the Jewish people. Of course, like Catholicism for the French, our religion is an aspect of our condition as
a people. But I am not a believer in the God who talks to us in
the Bible. Our essence is our Jewish peoplehood. Abraham,
Isaac, Jacob—these are the persons who started our family, our
people. In sum, the total Jew belongs to our people simply by
virtue of living in a Jewish land.

There is no inner necessity to express this totality through religious observances. I simply cannot believe in a God or a Christ
or a Mohammed. This sort of believing cannot be the basis of
Jewish identity.

HC: Well, I think it is hard to overlook that the essence of our
specifically Jewish culture would seem more than anything else
to be our religion. Nevertheless, I don't believe I insisted that a
Jew must be conventionally religious to be authentic, did I?

ABY: Perhaps not, but I still maintain that the goal, the aim of
totality is achieved through a total conjunction of peoplehood, a
natural participation in the whole culture so that we don't have
to choose, the way that Jews in the Diaspora must. *They*, per-

haps, are a chosen–choosing people, but we Israelis don't have to be.

HC: Nevertheless, thanks to your religious background, you possess enough knowledge to choose whether or not to choose. The same is true of Carmi or Yehuda Amichai. What about many of the younger, almost deracinated Israeli writers like some associated with the Tel Aviv School of poets? Things Jewish seem almost extirpated from their work. Their style is consciously international and, as Carmi has noted, deficient in specific Jewish resonance.

ABY: I must differ with you. Our culture undergoes continual change. The novels of Appelfeld, the poems of Amichai—these for me take the place of religion at the very center of Jewish culture. But so too does the work of the younger writers. Jewish experience is composed of a constant symbiosis between past and present. It is all legitimate. You know, if Balzac had read Camus or Sartre, he might well have exclaimed that they were not sufficiently French—or even French at all! But Camus is no less French for the French today than are Balzac or Stendhal.

HC: That's true, of course. Still it sounds to me as though you would substitute "Israelism" or some such thing for Judaism. Can't we plainly see the effect of such a tendency among our *yordim* once they settle in the Diaspora? Since the large majority of them are non-religious, they maintain little or no involvement with the local Jewish communities. They have nothing but their Hebrew, their Israeli origins, and their accents to keep them from getting swallowed up whole, like minnows in a whale. And these saving factors will be inoperative for their children.

ABY: Yes, that is true. Which is exactly why I have argued that the Jewish attachment for the Diaspora is a kind of neurosis. It is an attraction for the borderline, for the marginal existence that it sustains. Jews should certainly choose normalcy and come to live here . . . as you did.

HC: This idea of the border country plays, I think, a pivotal role in much of your fiction. There is the "borderline son" in your much-acclaimed novella *The Continuous Silence of a Poet*; Jerusalem itself in "Three Days and a Child"; elsewhere as well. Is your point that the border country is dangerous ground, a scene of psychological or physical conflict?

ABY: Yes, that is so. But really, I would like for myself to forget about borders, to be exempt from their influence. Jews are afraid to be alone by themselves. For thousands of years now, it has been the essential Jewish experience to inhabit one or another frontier. The Jew has defined himself against this frontier terrain which stands between himself and the non-Jew.

No matter how comfortable it has seemed, the Diaspora for the Jew has always been somewhat unfocused. Melville, for example, deals centrally with Americanness, but with Bellow the very ground shifts to examining just how it is that he is American at all. And then how it is that he is a Jew. In Israel alone resides the Jewish potential for getting beyond the margin-land, the border zone. And this is why the Jewish religion tends to undermine Israeli nationhood. Religious Jews are more sure of their identity. They actually can live securely as Jews in Brooklyn. So they need not stay in Israel.

HC: Excuse me, but don't the facts oppose your theorizing? *Yerida* is not a particularly religious phenomenon. Without question, most *yordim* are secular Jews. Moreover, in recent years a much higher proportion of religious rather than non-religious *olim* stick it out here.

ABY: No, there is also a religious *yerida*. Anyway, we are talking about numbers far too small for significant percentages. Among the few thousand *olim* who come every year, a hundred this way or that make for an insubstantial conclusion.

HC: Perhaps so. I understand that you have recently returned from the United States. Were you there on sabbatical?

ABY: Not on sabbatical. I was attending a conference in Vermont. Saul Bellow invited me. He heads the Center for Social and Intellectual History at the University of Chicago. Twelve writers came—myself, Czeslaw Milosz from Berkeley, Andrei Sinyavsky, others—all of us engaged in social and political activism. We discussed the writer's role in the larger world. One thing I became aware of was the strength of the New Right in America. It was frightening. My earlier experience in the States had been in the Sixties. What a difference!

HC: You, of course, are politically on the Left and well-known as a dove. Do you truly believe that peace between Israel and the Arab world is currently possible?

ABY: Of course, and especially after the peace treaty with Egypt, more and more must we prepare for peace. When finally the Arabs are ready, there must be no question about us.

HC: Just last week President Nimeiri of Sudan [deposed in 1985] urged the Arab world to abandon their past illusions about Israel and to deal with us as a permanent reality in this region.

ABY: Exactly, and even if what we live in is a smaller nation rather than a binational one, we would be better off with clearly defined borders. *Gush Emunim* [Jewish nationalist organization committed to settling and keeping the territory occupied by Israel in the 1967 war] live in the midst of another people. It is like Abraham creating his family again in the womb of another nation. What kind of compulsion or neurosis is this?

As for myself, I don't want forever to be concerned with how we Jews are different. Zionism is a proper reaction to this abnormalcy . . . or it is nothing. Yes, I believe that we can divide this land and that peace can finally be achieved. I shall tell you something more. Before 1967, Jerusalem was really a unique city. Small, divided Jerusalem had more of a Jewish character than the whole of Jerusalem today.

HC: Haifa has, of course, a substantial non-Jewish population and relatively little friction between its Arab and Jewish inhabitants. Might it serve as any sort of a model for us?

ABY: Haifa is a symbol of a good and proper balance. There is a small Arab minority that feels at home here because it *knows* that it is a minority. Aside from one or two actors, I personally have no Arab friends. In general, I don't seek out friends anyway. But whereas Haifa's Arabs don't exactly feel "occupied," still, how much better it would be for them were there a Palestinian State that would be their center. It wouldn't create a need for them to move there, but it would greatly enhance their self-respect. In general, things would function better.

HC: You mention actors. Your writing has shifted over the years from symbolic shorter fiction to novels that are psychologically dense. But you have also written for the stage: *A Night in May, Last Treatment,* some other plays. How do they fit in?

ABY: For me it is curious. I have had to pass through drama in order to move from short stories to longer fiction. The theater has been something of an intermediate stage for me. My problem was to enlarge the scope and number of my characters. For the stage they have to speak in their own voices. It has been a means to experiment with a larger number of voices.

HC: Family relationships, usually abrasive, have been at the center of your work from the start.

ABY: Yes. In some of the early, perhaps more allegorical stories, there are children separated from their parents, but as my own personal life has revolved more around my own family, naturally my fiction has also been more concerned with it. I am now working on my first novel which will span the several generations of a single family. Family, after all, is really the seed of the people.

HC: Yes, in both *A Late Divorce* and *The Lover* you seem to use it as a figure, almost a trope for the conflict and disintegration of Israel as a whole.

ABY: In a way, but these works are really not intended primarily as symbolic. They mean to reflect our psychological reality.

HC: I understand, but I'm also rather confused. Coming from California, where the majority of households have experienced divorce, I find Israeli family life, at least as it presents itself to

my eyes, to be remarkably stable. That is somewhat at variance
with the picture you present.

ABY: Well, perhaps I do present the extremities in the disintegration of the family, but as Freud has taught us, we can often
better comprehend the normal through a representation and ex-
amination of the extremes. There are, I think, two basic kinds of
literature. One tries to portray reality by constructing it. The
second endeavors to understand it by dismantling it. I could, for
example, try to teach my son about the mechanism of a clock by
building one with him from a diagram. Or we could take one
apart. Tolstoy is a builder; Dostoevsky a dismantler. I belong to
the school of Dostoevsky: I work in reverse. But I recognize that
the greater literature is made by the builders.

HC: What is your view of the current, strange political situation?

ABY: A mess, isn't it? There must, of course, be a National
Unity Government, and so with other writers I signed that open
letter urging such a step. The only alternative would have been
yet another election and more madness. And, of course, Mapam
[Socialist Left Party] and Yossi Sarid [Member of Israeli Par-
liament who left the Labor Party to join the Citizens Rights
Party] have fallen away, which weakens us in dealing with the
expansionists.

The Israeli Left has a sorry history of purists who prefer being
holier than thou. So *they* are pure, but Israel needs a government. There is no choice. And perhaps, when we finally have
used up all other choices, we will get ourselves clear of the territories—our preoccupation and our burden.

HC: In *Between Right and Right*, you wrote that you would prefer it, were Israel to abridge or curtail the privilege of Jews
abroad to come here as automatic citizens or to have any special
prerogatives in regard to our Jewish State unless they come on
aliya by a certain date.

ABY: Yes. As I said, we are the world's greatest experts on exile.
But our people must be *here* or the nation suffers and may fall.

We must draw the line. Jews elsewhere must decide who they really are. Ours is a need to stop running.

HC: Yet it seems to me that Yehuda in *A Late Divorce* and Gabriel in *The Lover* both are proto-*yored* [emigrant] figures for whom Israel serves as a trap they struggle unsuccessfully, at times comically, to leave behind. Both characters are drawn, I would say, with considerable sympathy.

ABY [smiling]: Yes, it is true. I understand them.

HC: I see. Just one last, niggling matter relating to your work. There occurs in it repeatedly a garage mechanic as a figure of authority. He may be found all the way back in your early story "A Long Hot Day" and as recently as *The Lover*. Just what might the curious critic make of him?

ABY: I suppose that I have great respect for someone who can make a car run. Now that I have a better car, perhaps the character of the garageman will play a smaller role in my work.

HC: I now must make my way to my own authority figure—the Egged bus driver—and begin my return journey home. Thank you very much.

Afterward I much regretted that, though I had given proper heed to Chaim Goldberg, Roni Brown's injunction had totally slipped my mind.

Yehuda Amichai

Neither Prophet nor Guru

Two weeks before Hanukkah, near the close of 1984, the early winter sun over Jerusalem was weak but the sky was clear. I entered the city's renovated Yemin Moshe quarter, a complex of posh, adjoining flats (many of them owned by part-time North American residents), which were laid out on a hillside just below one of the city's most famous landmarks, the Montefiore windmill. It was time for my 11 A.M. appointment to meet with poet Yehuda Amichai, Israel's most celebrated living poet. Six volumes of his poems and several collections of his short stories have been translated into English. In 1982 he was awarded the Israel Prize for Literature.

I felt pleasantly agitated. Six months earlier, in my review of a prose collection by poet Philip Larkin, I had noted the irony that "among Israeli writers . . . I read new stories by poet Yehuda Amichai with greater eagerness than anyone else's." Something similar was the case with this interview as well, but it nearly did not come off at all.

Several telephone attempts to arrange an appointment for an earlier date had proved fruitless. Finally, this occasion was set, but when I tried to confirm it by telephone the evening before, I could get nothing but busy signals and wrong numbers. At the appointed hour, I simply appeared at Amichai's house and knocked on the door. A tall, gray-haired, pleasant-faced woman escorted me into a dining area where I discovered the poet before a table peeling potatoes into a large pot.

Haim Chertok: Shalom. [The man looked at me quizzically.] I'm Haim Chertok. [Pause] We have an appointment for today . . . for now . . . for an interview.
Yehuda Amichai: Was there really an appointment for today?
HC: Well . . . yes. There was. That is, there *is*!
YA: There must be some confusion. I do remember it now, but I don't much like to give interviews.
HC: I am sorry. I made the appointment ten days ago. It's to be one of a series of literary interviews I've been publishing irregu-

larly in the *Jewish Frontier,* the Labor Zionist monthly [now bi-monthly] in New York. Here's the first one, my interview with Aharon Appelfeld [*JF*, March 1984]. I tried to reach you by telephone last night to confirm it, but I couldn't get through. If you prefer, I suppose I could just leave. I'm really very sorry.

YA: No. No, please come in. You'll just have to give me a few minutes while I finish up here. Please sit down in there.

I entered a large room which offered a panoramic view of the stony Hinnom—the Valley of Gehenna. Sitting prominently on the far side of the valley was the cross-crested, sprawling Dormition Abbey. While Amichai finished peeling his bowl of potatoes, I settled myself comfortably at a large, square, wooden table. On the walls of the ample room were some framed sketches. There were bookshelves, but smaller and fewer than one might have expected. Furnishings were modest, functional—not, I thought, unlike Amichai's writing style. After ten minutes, the bushy-browed poet entered the room with a smile and seated himself.

YA: Go right ahead and ask what you like.

HC: Thank you. The view from here is marvelous. I know that you spent your boyhood in Würzburg and arrived in Palestine in the 1930s at the age of twelve. Is your recollection of Germany distinct?

YA: Oh yes, certainly. Würzburg was one of the major centers of Jewish Orthodoxy in Southern Germany. A very close, warm, pleasant world it was.

HC: Würzburg was also a major target for Allied bombs during World War II.

YA: Yes, but it has been rebuilt almost exactly as it was before. It is still a very beautiful place, and the surrounding countryside is unchanged. I learned Hebrew as a boy growing up in Würzburg. We came to Palestine in 1935. I did not dislike our life in Würzburg. Nevertheless, my whole family, fortunately, came here in 1935.

HC: In one of the possible directions taken in your open-ended novel *Not of This Time, Not of This Place,* Joel, the protagonist, makes a return visit to Germany. Have you yourself ever returned?

YA: Yes, about fifteen years ago.

HC: However, in the alternative course of events in that novel, Joel remains in Israel and enjoys a brief affair with an American woman. Do the seemingly contradictory chains of events in that novel reflect your own ambivalence about making such a return voyage to the Germany of your childhood?

YA: Yes, just that. I returned for a visit, and the novel was one of the results. The trip gave me the push for writing the novel. [Pause] Yes, a psychological ambivalence, you could say. The two directions of the narrative aim at that. But you know, if one can pursue two courses simultaneously, why not a dozen? An infinite number? It verges on a sort of science fiction. But I have always been fascinated by doubles, split personalities, and alternative possibilities. A psychiatrist would make much of this, I'm sure. A great deal of doubleness may be found in the poems as well, of course. Perhaps even duplicity.

HC: In the end, did you as an adult discover in Würzburg what you had anticipated?

YA: It was very fine. You see, all of my family—ten uncles, everyone—came to Palestine some fifty years ago. I lost no one close during the war, so returning to Würzburg was just like returning to the scene of my childhood after thirty or more years. It was, in a way, a marvelous experience.

HC: Yes, I do understand. Last year I returned to visit the neighborhood in New York—the Bronx—where I spent my boyhood for the first time in fifteen years. In fact, I felt moved to write a short memoir about it.

YA: Your family is also from Germany?

HC: No, from Poland and Russia. On my father's side it's the Sharett family; my grandfather was Moshe Sharett's [Israel's first Foreign Minister and second Prime Minister] uncle.

YA: Ha! Briefly, in the 1930s, I shared a violin teacher with his journalist son . . .

HC: . . . Kobi [diminutive for Jacob].

YA: Yes, Kobi. [Laughs.] We learned the same Vivaldi concerto.

HC: I'm in much closer contact with his daughter, Yael Medini. She's married to an American. She too is a writer.

YA: Where will your Bronx memoir appear?

HC: In *Midstream*, this coming January or February, I think [in fact, June/July 1986 was when it finally saw publication].

YA: Midstream has moved far to the right. It's too bad. The editor there used to be Shlomo Katz, the man who translated *Not of This Time, Not of This Place.*

HC: I hadn't taken note of the translator, but I think he did an excellent job. But you know, besides Hardy, Lawrence, maybe Melville, not very many writers have been equally adept at poetry and prose. I remember feeling embarrassed for Faulkner when once I came across his youthful poetry. *Not of This Time, Not of This Place* is such a fine novel, why haven't you written others?

YA [smiling]: But I have. I have written *two* novels.

HC: Oh! [Pause] The second must not be translated.

YA: True. Basically, though, I am a poet largely because poetry verges closely on mythic power. Rachel, for example, is not really buried at the site of what in Bethlehem we call "Rachel's Tomb." Nevertheless, that too is the correct site. The fool is the one who insists on his truth to the exclusion of others. And after all, truth, beauty, the very meaning of words—all these are relative values. This is the realm of poetry.

However, you could also say that I am a poet as the result of laziness. I am too lazy to write more prose than I do. Prose is like making love to one woman instead of to fifty, which you can do with poetry.

HC: This may seem like an odd question, but when you are struck by a literary idea, do you consciously decide to treat it in a poem, a story, or a novel?

YA: Oh no. It's not that deliberative. Writing should always be a pleasure, spontaneous—like making love. Not so manipulative.

By the way, did you know that Appelfeld started as a poet?

HC: When we talked, he passed over his poetry quickly.

YA: He doesn't talk about his poems, but they weren't bad.

HC: You recently have published a new collection of poems, *Great Tranquillity: Questions and Answers.*

YA: Yes, both in Hebrew and in English.

HC: The review in *The Jerusalem Post* was not very friendly. You were accused of leaning on old stylistic mannerisms.

YA: Yes, well the *Post* is mostly politics, you know. Who-knows-whom and all that. It got a very good notice in *The New York Times.*

HC: You have recently returned from a visit to America, am I right?

YA: Yes. I had been there many times for shorter periods. I taught for a period at the University of California, Berkeley. But this last year, when I was teaching Creative Writing at N.Y.U., was my longest visit. I enjoy America. Both in Jewish and in academic circles, my work is well-known there.

HC: Any dominant impressions?

YA: Well, America *is*, after all, the only Jewish community outside of Israel that is surviving. British Jewry is stagnant, dying. Then there are the French, of course, but in the Diaspora only in America is there open Jewish dialogue, vitality. Its Jewish community is thriving and will, I feel, survive. Sometimes, perhaps, it moves in the wrong direction. But it is self-confident and alive. Many people retain their Jewish identity despite marrying non-Jews. I myself have seen it. [Smiling] Perhaps you don't agree, but the mixed marriages they have there are not all that bad. We Israelis tend to patronize American Jewry. Why not instead be happy about it? American Jews accept their Jewishness. I feel, in fact, that we in Israel could learn a little something from this—the better to enjoy our being Jewish.

HC: Yes. Well, I of course chose some years ago to depart from America, and I confess to feeling less enthusiasm than you for the state of American Jewry. After his recent year in Boston, Appelfeld also expressed feelings very different from yours.

YA: It could be fairly said that I disagree with the old, false romanticism about Judaism. In practice, Orthodox Judaism can keep you busy nearly all of the time with things you should be doing. Keeps you feeling guilty. But feeling Jewish should also feel pleasurable. What can be wrong with that?

HC: As long as you're asking, my own experience in the fields of America has yielded a different impression. My wife, myself, and our two children lived in Central California where, from the time of the Gold Rush, Jews were among the first non–Spanish-speaking settlers. But most of that first wave's descendants are Jews no longer. And probably neither are those of the subsequent wave. The handwriting on the wall seemed sufficiently clear. Coming on *aliya,* living in Israel was for us a conscious survival choice as Jews, and even more so for our children. In fact, we now have two additional children that we probably would not have had had we remained in California, the capital of the Kingdom of Self-Gratification.

YA [smiling]: Perhaps I was being a bit provocative. You did choose the right way. I myself tell people that Israel is the only place that Jews can live where they don't have always to be thinking about being Jewish. For, as you are aware, the practice of Judaism is, in practice, impractical for many of us Jews.

HC: Perhaps that's just what makes it all the more attractive to others of us. May I turn to a different subject? Like most Israeli writers, you have been an academic for most of your life, is that correct?

YA: Yes, but not just now. Though I still teach a few hours a week at Hebrew University and at Hebrew Union College, last year I took an early retirement. And I was never really a proper "academic." I taught Creative Writing. All that I have is a B.A. degree. I taught for fifteen years in the public schools, then for fifteen years more at Hayim Greenberg Teachers College. I enjoyed teaching, yes, but my primary purpose was to make a living.

When I was eighteen, I joined the British army for four years. I served in Egypt and the western desert: Palestinian [Jewish!] units were kept distant from combat zones. After that came a year in the Hagana [pre-State Israeli army], mainly smuggling arms. Such experience makes one wonder how someone like Reagan, who has never been under fire, can order others to fight and shoot. It's crazy! Immoral!

Anyway, after the War of Independence I took a concentrated course to learn to be a teacher. Actually, I started writing quite late in life.

HC: How do you perceive the current literary situation in Israel? Are there any significant changes from how it was when you first began to write and publish?

YA: You know, in Israel poetry is more at the center of things than in America where it's read only in the major academic centers and a few other special locales. Also aloud: we don't have the public readings here. I enjoy giving public readings of my work but only in translation. Then it's not quite mine any longer, and I can enjoy it more.

Here in Israel, of course, every generation backs away from its parents. Rebels against the old. That has always been the case, and not here alone. Take, for example, Dylan Thomas, now largely ignored. You may be sure that in a few years some Yale professor will rediscover his genius.

But I've always kept away from the so-called literary scene, from current fashions. Really, I write for my own pleasure, for my own enjoyment. It's been that way from the very beginning. I have never been involved in any circle or group. In a sense, my politics is in my poetry; it *is* my poetry. Slogan poetry, the kind written out of guilt, is bad poetry. It just coddles the poet's ego, makes him think that he's done something. But my politics are, in reality, involved in my every poem.

HC: Perhaps just a shade more prosaically, might you state what is your present political stance?

YA: Oh, I've spoken a few times at Peace Now rallies. I am generally against the right wing taking over. But I think I exert more influence, such as it is, through my poems than I would by espousing public positions.

HC: In your poems you frequently address God and often in sarcastic tones as in "O God Full of Compassion" and "God Has Pity on Schoolchildren." Whom or what are you addressing?

YA: Oh, call it God, Mankind, History, some higher power. The word doesn't matter much, does it? "God" is easiest for a Jew. What is important is the manner in which men and women treat their fellow men and women. What is stupid is the nonsense about whether ancient bones are buried beneath the hotel that the ultra-Orthodox are trying to prevent getting built in Tiberias.

HC: Many of your best-known poems—say, "If I Forget Thee O Jerusalem," "Patriotic Reflections"—revolve about a tension between the national or patriotic dimension versus the personal or private. The poetic voice seems torn between—trapped.

YA: Yes. Well, that tension is my own, of course. It will never, I suppose, be finally resolved, but my answer to the world is that my life is here in Israel with my wife and three children. Whenever, wherever I travel, I meet *yordim* by the dozens. But as I said earlier, Israel is the only place to be a Jew and not have continually to think about it. Still, it must of course be recognized that one's practical, daily life is not the same as an ideology.

Perhaps what's involved here can best be seen in the contrasting approaches between the Eastern and Western, the Sephardim and Ashkenazim. The Ashkenazic West is more ideological; the Sephardim are, I think, more easy, more human. They don't disown their own because of a football game on Shabbat. Of course I am not talking about Shas [ultra-Orthodox Sephardi Torah Guardians Party]; they're just political gangsters. The

problem is that the politicians—Shulamit Aloni, Yossi Sarid
[left-wing members of Israel's Parliament], all of them—have
cushy jobs on the side. They don't *truly* feel responsible for rep-
resenting voters, the citizens.

HC: That is one of the hardest things for an American immigrant
to become accustomed to here. The Washington representative
from our district in California had his limitations, but he was
famous for looking out for the interests of his constituents. And
he really did help. Here there is often no one to whom to turn.

YA: Exactly. In Israel your vote has nothing to do with the out-
come of an election. Unlike in America, here alienation is built
right into the system. But to return to the Sephardim, their good
side is that although they may hate each other, they manage to
live together . . .

HC: Yes, my experience living in Yeroham, which is predominantly Sephardi, bears that out.

YA: . . . but some of the right-wing Ashkenazim are really psy-
chopaths. It seems to me that I've heard something about there
being a college down in Yeroham?

HC: Yes, there is. A small one—Ramat Hanegev [Negev Hills].
Until not long ago, I did some teaching there.

YA: I would be happy to come to Yeroham to talk to the students
there. Now that I am "retired," I can use my time as I please. I
think I would enjoy that. I like the desert very much.

HC: Wonderful. I'll try to arrange things. I'm sure that they will
be delighted. But a final question dealing with your poetry: in
one of your poems I most admire, "Jerusalem 1967," the speaker
stops at the shop of an Arab on Yom Kippur. Do you have any
Arab friends?

YA: Some acquaintances, but no real friends. Just now, it seems,
isn't the right time for close relations between Arabs and Jews.

HC: I recently read a sociological study purporting to show that
of all the major ethnically split-up cities—Montreal, Beirut,
Belfast—none is quite as hermetically divided as Jerusalem.

YA: I am opposed to our keeping all of the West Bank. It's plain that the time has not yet come for Arabs and Jews to be together. All that I really want is to live in a Jewish State. It's a remarkable paradox: the Left is now for policies which would separate the communities while the very far Right, living right there in the occupied territories, are in reality working for integration. Left and Right have exchanged positions, turned completely around. A true paradox!

But you know, all such abstractions are relative. What is the "beautiful"? Instead of a sunset or a flower, today it could be a jet plane. Words inflate like money: the more they're printed, the more value they lose.

HC: Do you ever ponder what seems to have gone wrong here in Israel?

YA: Oh, I don't like to complain. We now *have* our Jewish State. The reality is far from the ideal. The Jewish people have married Israel, this land. But as in a real marriage, things have cooled down. Complaining about it sounds like an old man complaining about his age. An old couple should just live together. That's all. It is, after all, perfectly normal. We have, after all, passed the honeymoon stage, passed the romance, but this is, nonetheless, a true marriage. Such is my Zionism.

I am, you see, beyond illusions. In America people, without the slightest intention of doing so, every year repeat "Next year in Jerusalem." Now *that* is what I call true cynicism.

HC: You may now be quasi-retired, but you don't at all sound ready to stop working. Nevertheless, you can look back on much of a lifetime of significant achievement and many awards. What projects have you yet in mind? What do you still want to accomplish?

YA: Oh, to continue with my own thing with poetry: to clean up the language, to use it the right way. I have no wish to be a prophet or a guru. As always, I shall use my own life as my material. You know, I have never been a poet in the professional sense. It's been that way all my life, and so it should remain.

HC: Do your own children write?

YA: My boy, who is twelve, likes to paint. He's the bohemian in the family. I have a girl who is six. And then my twenty-three-year-old son, though he likes to write as well, does economics and computer science. So my children are not growing up in competition with their father. They have the normal oedipal conflicts, of course, but not, at least, that one.

As if on cue, Amichai's twelve-year-old son entered at the front door all out of sorts with some school problem. The celebrated poet instantly was transformed into just another father of a troubled young adolescent.

HC: This is obviously an appropriate point for me to be off. For someone who does not enjoy giving interviews, you have been very kind and forthcoming.

YA: Oh really, it was nothing. I fully enjoyed it.

HC: Well, especially after our initial confusion, I appreciate it. I shall look into the details of inviting you down for a visit to our exotic Yeroham. I'll contact you about it.

YA: Good. Really, it was my pleasure. You must come again. Next time bring your wife and children.

I made my way up the hill toward the windmill and soon was riding the bus to my home in the desert. Two months later, true to his word, Amichai came down to Yeroham to spend a day with students at the local college and high school. He scored a major success with them. Under the title "Of Poetry and Prejudice," my account of his visit (which, by chance, almost coincided with one by Meir Kahane) later appeared in the monthly periodical Moment.

Dan Pagis

Some Sort of Abel

*Because the passages and turnings of the ship-like structure con-
taining the poet's office at Hebrew University's Mount Scopus campus in Jerusalem were so notoriously labyrinthine, I was a quarter
of an hour late for our meeting. Rising from his desk as I entered,
Dan Pagis greeted me with courtly warmth. A broad-shouldered,
manifestly gentle man in his mid-50s, he was evidently at the
prime of his life and powers. He responded to my questions in excellent, lightly-accented English in an expansive manner, tending kindly to embellish as though in thoughtful anticipation of
what he thought I might want to hear. In this he was generally—
though not always—correct.*

His published collections of poems include The Shadow Dial
(1959), Late Leisure *(1964),* Transformations *(1970), and* Brain
*(1976). Two selections of his poems have appeared in English
translation: the first was a joint volume with T. Carmi (Carcanet
Press, 1972, later reissued as a Penguin); the second,* Points of
Departure, *appeared under the imprint of the Jewish Publication
Society in 1983. Both received fine notices.*

*Our meeting occurred late in the afternoon of an overcast day
in February of 1985.*

Haim Chertok: I'm very sorry that I'm late. Even knowing the
room number and building color code for this wing, it wasn't
easy to find the right corridor. What an awkward building to
negotiate!
Dan Pagis: Yes, you're right. I taught for many years at the
Givat Ram campus of the university [in West Jerusalem]. Such a
cheerful campus, which for me also holds pleasant memories of
my student days. I have never felt as comfortable here at Mount
Scopus.
HC: Quite a few younger writers nowadays seem to work at
newspapers, but like many Israeli writers of your generation,
you are a full-fledged academic. How significant is this to your
sense of yourself as a poet and as a writer?

DP: Yes. Well, my field of specialization is Medieval Hebrew Poetry; in fact, later, pre-modern Hebrew poetry as well. This covers a very extensive period: the Palestinian and Eastern poetry in Byzantium and early Islamic times, the Golden Age in Spain that runs from around 1000 through the fifteenth century, and also several other centers. In Italy, for example, Hebrew poetry reflected various styles including the Renaissance and the Baroque. It extended from after the Enlightenment right up to the nineteenth century. What we're talking about is more than a thousand years of poetry.

HC: Yes, but really I am more interested in how your role as a medievalist affects your idea of yourself as a poet. In the United States, many poets, novelists, and dramatists take academic appointments as writers-in-residence. Or perhaps they teach occasional courses in Creative Writing, perform public readings, sometimes teach contemporary literature. Much of this is neither full-time nor permanent; nor, if I may say so, is it often all that very serious. Your situation, like that of many other prominent Israeli writers—Yehoshua, Carmi, others—is not at all comparable.

DP: That is true. The situation in Israel for writers is quite different; at least, my own personal situation is. I have something of a split personality, but I'm not aware that I suffer from it. My job here has no connection with my poetry. I am here in this office, a medieval scholar, pure and simple, with a shelf-load of scholarly papers—which alone count here. Hebrew University is very strict in that way. Like everyone else, I have had to produce solid contributions to my field. I think that perhaps Haifa University and Tel Aviv University might well be more flexible places at which a creative writer could work.

But the situation at Hebrew University well suits an important and genuine interest of mine: deciphering Baroque and Renaissance historical backgrounds. Scholarship is what I *do*, you know. It—the Hebrew literature of this vast period—really appeals to me. It has nothing to do, however, with my own poetry or my theory of poetry. You know, I published my first poems before I became a student and long before I decided to become a scholar. Yet it would not have been congenial for me to teach modern literature—the work of my friends and colleagues. I truly cannot imagine it.

Did you know that here at Hebrew University we have some first-rate scientists who are also fine poets?

HC: No, I didn't. Like who?

DP: There are Avraham Huss, Avner Treiner, Shlomo Weiner. Some others as well. They too, I suppose, are split personalities.

HC: Then as a poet are you wholly uninfluenced by your studies of the poetry of Yehuda Halevi [12th century, Spain], Ibn Gabirol, and Immanuel of Rome?

DP: That is correct. I think that an article dealing with physics or genetics would have a greater chance of influencing my poetry. Except for one occasion, I don't recall ever making an allusion to medieval poetry in my own verse, and that single allusion is from a period which I don't usually teach. It isn't that I have any inhibitions about it. It just doesn't happen.

HC: Then whom among the Europeans and moderns could you cite as having had a significant influence on your poetry? I'm virtually certain, for example, that I can perceive John Donne's "Canonization" hovering above the coin image in your fine poem "A New Lover" as well as the shadow of Kafka in the given situation of "Dossier Zero."

DP [pointing behind him]: Yes, Donne is right here on my shelf. As for Kafka, that surely wouldn't be unusual. Anyway, German is my first language. Before the war I had no formal schooling whatsoever. When I arrived in Israel in 1946, I didn't know any Hebrew. [Pause] Still, I did publish my first poems only three years later.

HC: What were your early Israeli years like?

DP: I had been in the camps for some years during the war, and when I came to Israel on Youth Aliya [rescue operation that brought unattached young Jews from Europe to Israel], I was sent to live on Kibbutz Merhavya. Like everyone else, I worked hard, but we were fortunate in having good teachers. In those days my Hebrew was too meager for me to be affected by any Hebrew writers. The major influence on my first published collection of poetry, *The Shadow Dial*, was German poetry, especially Rilke.

Later, I attended the teacher's seminary of my kibbutz movement and, while I was working on my doctorate at Hebrew University, I taught for some years at Kibbutz Gat. By the time of my second book, *Late Leisure*, in 1964, I was under the influence of more contemporary voices: the Yugoslav Popa, the Czech Miroslav Holub, and especially the Pole Zbigniew Herbert. I learned to read English on my own, largely from detective novels. By the time I had reached university, I could handle it well.

HC: Did or do you experience any problems, that is, emotional problems, in reading German?

DP: Oh no!

HC: Your background sounds very similar to that of Aharon Appelfeld, your neighbor in Mevasseret Zion, where I've heard that you reside: Holocaust experience, no early formal schooling, Youth Aliya, academic career.

DP: Yes, we are about the same age—I was born in 1930—and have had similar experiences. I came from a place in Bukovina Province, now divided between Rumania and the Soviet Union, just twenty miles from him. But for many years I did not write about those experiences. He could much sooner; in fact, from the very first.

HC: Because of your prominence in the field of Medieval Hebrew, I would like to ask you something about which I also asked Carmi. In his review of Carmi's *Anthology of Hebrew Poetry*, the eminent American critic Harold Bloom argues that, because the poetic elements in the Bible weren't properly conceived of or perceived as "poetry," Hebrew poetry lacks a genuine poetic tradition. His chief authority is the recent, highly acclaimed study by James Kugel, *The Idea of Biblical Poetry* put out by Yale.

DP: This and similar views I've encountered seem to me very, very wrong. I worked closely with Carmi for years on his anthology, and, I might add, was most pleased when he dedicated it to me. I worked on it, as I say, because I really believe in both the variety and the continuity of Hebrew poetry. Moreover, I discussed the issue with Kugel himself when he visited Israel. I believe that his theory has to do with the common conception of poetry, or of its employment, in the absence of abstract formal theory. That the Bible is largely poetic, however, may be immediately apprehended by almost any reader. Further, the matter is explicit in talmudic literature where the question of the appreciation of metaphorical language and its use in connection with the Bible is discussed.

Of course, it may be assumed that language has a liturgical function, but perhaps it would be well to see as mere romantic prejudice the notion that poetry intended for liturgical or social use should not be considered poetry at all. Modern poetry itself, among other uses, has a social function. For Bloom to deny either the poetic value or, as Kugel puts it, the "idea" of poetry to the Psalms seems somewhat restrictive to me. It is *not* anachronistic to call them poetry. Quite the contrary.

HC: It seems to me that a typical Dan Pagis poem is often recognizable by its resolution through the outside, imperative voice. I'm thinking now of "Go, You are not allowed to forget" at the ending of "Instructions for Crossing the Border"; of "quiet . . ." at the close of "Draft of a Reparations Agreement"; of the "Don't worry. Don't worry" that ends "Brothers"; and many others as well. It's an off-stage voice, like that of a film director, and it impinges upon the situation of each poem.

DP: Honestly, I never thought of that. But come to think of it, it does seem to apply to quite a number of my later poems. Now

comes the trickier part: what to make of it? And there I really
cannot analyze my own technique or its implications. That's
really not my job anyway, is it? The less important things—the
occasion for this poem or that—I probably could supply; the
other isn't my department.

[Avraham] Shlonsky [1900–1973], Nathan Alterman, Leah
Goldberg [1911–1970], though in many respects great modern-
ists, still wrote in a rich, poetic language. At first they much
affected me, but I haven't reprinted any of those more derivative
poems of mine in *Points of Departure*. My tendency has been to
use more and more colloquial language. Similarly, I have moved
from more formal, traditional patterns to more open forms. However, my latest Hebrew collection, *Double Exposure*, contains a
final section—"Out of Line"—consisting of prose poems. Free
verse is not, of course, a new development, but it feels like a
natural direction for me. As to *why* I feel this need, that, of
course, is another matter.

HC: What role does the Holocaust play in your poetry?

DP: Poetry is an extension of personal experiences, albeit often
in disguise. My poems of late have been increasingly autobiographical. I do at times feel like some sort of Abel figure. But is
that really so astonishing?

HC: You're referring now to your own experience in the Holocaust.

DP: Yes. Only in 1970, with the section "A Sealed Railway Car"
in *Gilgul* [*Transformations*] could I consciously refer to the Holocaust, albeit only on an archetypal plane, through the figures
of Cain, Adam, and Eve. Perhaps in two or three of the poems
the allusion is more direct, as in "Draft of a Reparations Agreement." Incidentally, some of my more bitter poems occasionally
get mentioned not because of their intrinsic value, but because
of their subject matter—the Holocaust, I mean.

Critics tend to ignore "Footprints" merely, I think, because it
is a longer poem. For that reason in *Points of Departure* I posi-
tioned it right after the shorter Holocaust poems. In "Footprints"

I attempted to come to terms with the problem of confronting the Holocaust and to go *beyond* bitterness and sarcasm. At first I hadn't included it in this relevant section.

HC: Let me pursue a collateral matter just a bit further. Your poem on the Hebrew-writing American poet Gabriel Preil, "The Grand Duke of New York," closes by citing his line, "Wrongs fade beyond the shore. . . ." The end of your "Instructions for Crossing the Border," however, strikes a contradictory note: "Go, You are not allowed to forget."

DP: Yes, but perhaps it's only natural to feel contradictory pressures. Anyway, the Preil poem is, of course, about New York. You know, I used to believe once that it was quite impossible to write about the Holocaust at all . . . until the subject forced itself upon me.

HC: It's odd. Lately it feels as though half the novels I get for review feature a survivor among their cast of characters. But then again, I suppose that the very fact that the Holocaust impinges on a book greatly increases the chance its publisher will send a review copy to *The Jerusalem Post* in the first place.

DP: As I said, for me it was only in 1970 that I felt compelled to return in my work to the war years, and even later—in my last book, in fact—to my origins in Bukovina. This has cost me a great deal, but evasion also exacts its price.

HC: Have you ever revisited Eastern Europe?

DP: Oh no. I would hate to go there.

HC: Where have you traveled outside of Israel?

DP: I've taken two, actually three trips to Western Europe—to my former dream countries of France and England. This came late, when I was twenty-five, twenty-eight, and thirty-four, but it opened up the world for me. I have been on sabbaticals to the States four times: to the Jewish Theological Seminary in New York, the University of California at San Diego and at Berkeley, and Harvard. And just now I have received an invitation to give a reading at the Library of Congress in Washington this coming April.

HC: Any notable impressions of America?

DP: In fact, yes. Visiting America had the effect of freeing up my poetry. When I visited with my aunt in Manhattan, I discovered my own childhood. She had preserved my uncle's room as it was during his lifetime: it was just like a room in Bukovina, in my grandparents' house. Suddenly I encountered this experience of the past. It helped me to open up.

When I first came to Israel, I had thought to put all that behind me. It was too painful. I even changed my name: Dan, of course, is Israeli. But New York evoked a personal dream, an American dream.

HC: Your America, even as a recollection or dream, reminds me of Kafka's fantasy of America—his Oklahoma Nature Theater.

DP: Yes, of course. Amazing. You know, before the war it had been possible for us to go to America. My aunt and uncle wanted us to come, but there was a delay, and after June '41 it was impossible for us to get out, even via Siberia and Shanghai. Then this happened, and I encountered my own Oklahoma Nature Theater in 1968–69 in New York.

HC: You must have been at Morningside Heights during the Columbia University student demonstrations?

DP: Yes, just a little later, but they didn't much affect me. More personally significant was that then I met Gabriel Preil, the great Hebrew portraitist of New York. In fact, I have written a series of poems about New York. Here they are [looking through rows of books on his shelves] . . . No, they're not here after all.

HC: Moyshe-Leyb Halpern, the Yiddish poet, also wrote a series on New York after his encounter with the city. So did Lorca, for that matter. Neither shared your enthusiasm. In the course of your visits, did you get any sense of American Jewish life, of its state of vitality or enervation?

DP: It seems to me that there is more interest than ever in the Jewish past. I'm judging from several encounters I had with youth groups. It seems an encouraging development.

HC: Here you differ from Appelfeld who formed a disheartening impression from his year of teaching at Brandeis and Harvard.

DP: Well, for me New York—also New England—is a place of magic. My personal dream of America is not yet over. It remains new, strange, and wonderful.

HC: Do you think of your poetry in purely personal terms, or does it carry a consciously political viewpoint as well?

DP: I suppose that individual poems may be seen to have a political coloring. I did, after all, grow up on a *Hashomer Hatza'ir* ["Young Guards," Left-Wing Socialist] kibbutz, and I've never abandoned that Weltanschauung. But my poems rarely verge on direct political commentary, except perhaps "Exercise in Practical Hebrew" in my second collection. It issued from events in the Yom Kippur War [1973] and from the election of 1977. Although it actually was written before the war in Lebanon, it was included in a recent anthology of war poems. I insisted, by the way, that this be indicated in the book.

HC: Does the performance of the coalition government under Shimon Peres seem hopeful to you so far?

DP: Other writers—A. B. Yehoshua, Amos Oz—are politically more active than I. Like all of us, however, I hope against hope that things will improve.

HC: The other evening I and a group of friends, mostly immigrants from America, were considering which conditions if any might lead to our departure from Israel. The prospect of, say, a Prime Minister Ariel Sharon could cause some of us seriously to reconsider what we were doing here.

DP: Oh no! Nothing could drive me away from here—save, perhaps, a new Holocaust. [Smiling] I am, you should know, a real Zionist. In actuality, I believe it is not possible for me to live elsewhere. This is where my children are. I have twins: a boy and a girl. They are both now serving in the army.

HC: Tell me, which of the younger Israeli poets do you read and particularly enjoy?

DP: I wouldn't want to mention some and skip over others. I will say this: sometimes I fail to perceive the *poetry* in the newer po-

etry. A blind spot, perhaps. But some of the younger people
seem to me magnificent.

HC: Your poems, like those of Gilboa, Amichai, others of your
generation, are laced with allusions to biblical motifs and Jewish themes. Many of the younger Israeli poets seem consciously
to avoid this material. Or perhaps, as Carmi responded to me, it
is simply inaccessible for them. But then, if that is the case,
what makes their poetry "Jewish" at all?

DP: Well, it is, after all, written in Hebrew.

HC: Is *that* it? Then what about the work of Anton Shammas
and a few other Israeli Arabs which is now being written in
Hebrew?

DP: Yes, there is a problem there. Still, I believe that the Jewish tradition is itself embedded in the Hebrew language. [Pause]
But you know, what I really think is that this skirting of Jewish
themes is a healthy trend. About eighty years ago, in 1905,
Bialik wrote a defense of poets who sought their own voices in
Hebrew. Poets do not have to be "engaged." I don't feel any guilt
about not producing political or "Jewish" poems, so I really
think that the present situation with the younger poets is a positive one.

In short, I have serious doubts about either religion or politics
in poetry. All programmatic poetry seems to me a kind of deple-
tion. What *does* bother me is not this: it is the shallowness I detect in the work of some of the younger generation of poets.

HC: You are not alone in that. I hope you enjoy your April trip to
Washington and that America remains a good dream.

DP [rising]: Thank you. I'll see you downstairs. Otherwise, you
might never find your way outside.

*Not long after our meeting, Dan Pagis learned that he was suf-
fering from cancer. His untimely death occurred in late July
of 1986.*

Shulamith Hareven

Miracle Hater

Panting from the steep, uphill climb to her building from the bus stop on the main street, I arrived at the apartment of Shulamith Hareven, one of the best-known and most highly respected Israeli writers, on a brightly sunlit morning in December 1985. Below, the Jerusalem street shimmered in squinty light. Rows of potted plants lined the ledge of her balcony; as one might expect, books were prominently featured in her living room.

In her 50s, Hareven displays a friendly, maternal manner: she smiles easily and is adept at putting a visitor at ease. She efficiently served tea and cookies and attended to household activities while we spoke.

Haim Chertok: That hike up the hill must help to keep you in good shape.

Shulamith Hareven: It is a bit of a climb. I hope you don't mind if I do my wash while we talk. After all our rain, I don't dare lose the opportunity of a sunny day.

HC: Of course not.

SH: I'm familiar with your town of Yeroham. My son lived there for a year when he was seventeen as a member of a *garin* [settlement group] that moved on from Yeroham. That must be twelve years ago. How did you come there?

HC: Oh, we were members of another *garin. Mashmia Shalom* [Proclaim Peace] we called ourselves—a passel of observant doves. Some have left, but most of us have remained and like it in Yeroham. My son is now about your son's age at that time he was in Yeroham. He's studying at a *hesder* yeshiva [seminary combining religious studies with military service].

Knowing Yeroham makes you a relatively rare bird among Jerusalemites. For many it could as well be on the moon. Tell me something about your upbringing.

SH: I was in the Hagana underground during the War of Independence and served as a teenage medic during the Siege of Jerusalem.

HC: You've skipped over quite a few years. You were born here?

SH: No.

HC [pause]: Okay. And then?

SH: I was one of the founders of *Galei Tsahal* [Army Network radio station]. It wasn't the round-the-clock station it is today. Then we were on three-and-a-half hours a day. I worked as well on *Kol Yisrael* [Voice of Israel radio station], and have always worked as a writer, essayist, and columnist.

HC: Where does your journalism appear?

SH: Mainly in *Yediot Ahronot* [Israel's most popular tabloid].

HC: Is your background religious?

SH: If you mean a study of the sources, yes, quite a bit. As for religious practice, no. I do have one grandfather who was a *hozer b'tshuva* [person who adopts religious observance, a "penitent"], but he is the only one in the family. My feeling is that at our present stage of Judaism, knowledge and creation within the culture have come to replace ceremony, just as ceremony and prayer, in their time, came to replace the sacrifices.

HC: And what about the range of your work as a writer?

SH: Let's see: two books of poetry; a novel—*City of Many Days*—that has been translated into English but is now out of print [she rummaged for a copy on a bookshelf and handed it to me]; three books of short stories and one of children's verse; a collection of essays—*The Dulcinea Syndrome*—that surprised everyone by becoming a Number One best seller. That's more or less it.

HC: More? Or less?

SH [laughs]: Well . . . less. There's also a thriller—*The Link*—that I originally published under an assumed name. No one guessed that a woman had written it. When my identity as the writer was revealed on a TV interview, there were some very red faces. Many reviewers had thought that a professional spy must have written it. What else am I up to? Here's the paperback edition of *City of Many Days*. [She grimaces at the half-dressed woman on the cover.] Terrible, isn't it? And oh yes, my story "Loneliness" represented Israel in an international anthology of stories by women which appeared in nine countries simultaneously in 1981.

Then there's my latest novella, *The Miracle Hater*, which identifies *midrash* [Jewish folk legend] with the re-creation of myth. It takes place during the Exodus from Egypt; the protagonist is a man who simply cannot comprehend or accept what is happening. The funny part is that while non-religious readers thought I was trying to explode myths, religious people knew perfectly well that I derived every scene in the book from an existing *midrash*.

HC: Hence the title?

SH: Hence the title. My protagonist is opposed to Moses' leadership and to the very idea of miracles. As I say, I think this is my best book so far, and although it was exceedingly difficult to translate, the job has already been done by the very best in the trade—Hillel Halkin.

HC: In his rational stance toward experience and rejection of the miraculous, might this distruster of miracles resemble one Shulamith Hareven?

SH: Well, I am very fond of him. In the novella, Moses is seen through the eyes of this skeptic who lives on the periphery of the camp, really the smallest of the small. Although he persists in demanding personal justice, all he and everyone else keep getting are a lot of miracles. In reality, he and Moses are the only true monotheists in the camp. It took me five years to develop a linguistic concept that *sounds* like biblical Hebrew but, in fact, is not. There's no way to convey that—its prime linguistic effect—in any translation. Hebrew, you know, is truly untranslatable. Incidentally, next week I'm to lecture at the Van Leer Institute. It's one of a series of lectures about new interpretations of Judaism. My subject is language as *midrash*.

Something else I suppose you should know is that I am the only woman member of the Academy of Hebrew Language.

HC: That's the Israeli version of the French Academy, isn't it? The policeman of Hebrew language purity?

SH: Not at all. We are really more involved in preserving linguistic norms in an immigrant country that has been inundated by all kinds of foreign influences. Our main work is lexicography, not as imposed from on high but by request. This year I sit on the committee of medicine and microbiology. Whenever professionals in these fields need advice in coining or appropriating new terms, we help them come up with something suitable in Hebrew.

HC: And how *is* the state of the tongue nowadays?

SH: In Israel, in spite of some undermining influences, still very good. To be sure, secularization has contributed to a definite loss of original idiom and phraseology, which is a pity. But it is still infinitely better than abroad. In the 2,000 years of *galut*, in every Jewish community at any given time, the majority of men— not, of course, of women—could read a Hebrew text. Nowadays, Western Jews are probably the first or second generation of Jews to have lost that capacity.

HC: Are you the first woman to sit on the Academy?

SH: No. I'm pretty sure that Leah Goldberg was also a member.

HC: Any other authorial activities you have omitted?

SH: Oh yes, one of my stories—"The Witness"—has just been adapted for the youth theater. You should try to see it.

HC: I shall. Let me focus more closely on a short novel and some stories from what I think is your particularly fine, still untranslated collection, *B'didut* [*Loneliness*].

SH [smiling]: Go right ahead, but don't expect me to tell you all that much.

HC: City of Many Days deals with Sephardic life in Jerusalem, material surely unfamiliar to most American readers. It seems to me a genuinely charming novel, a genre piece on the order of some recent South American fiction—say, that of Mario Vargas Llosa. It is quite different from your stories in *B'didut* where you deal with material much closer to actual or day-to-day life. The difference is reminiscent of the gap between the fictional worlds of American writers like Eudora Welty, on the one hand, and John Cheever on the other.

SH: Perhaps. [Smiles] I'm very fond of Cheever. In any event, that is the reader's problem.

HC: In the title story, "Loneliness," the solid, comfortable world of Dolly Jacobus suddenly disintegrates and her life becomes almost unbearable. Something similar occurs with the sudden, unexpected encounter that takes place in "A Couple of Hours on the Road." Most of your stories, in fact, seem to issue from a sudden estrangement from the surface of reality. Is your point that all seeming stability is illusory? Or is this actually intended as a reflection of specifically Israeli or perhaps Jewish reality?

SH: Well, I write about Israeli experience, and that experience, being so intense and concentrated, is probably a good background for distilling human experience anywhere. [The washer stops.] Excuse me while I hang up the clothes. Would you like a second cup of tea?

HC: Yes, thank you.

SH: And try the cookies. These are quite kosher, from the store.

HC [after a five-minute delay]: "The Witness" is, I think, a particularly effective story. (I persevere, you see.) In it you depict the incapacity of an Israeli teacher and his students to believe one young man's eye-witness account of what actually happened to his family in Europe during the Holocaust. Does this reflect something of your own sense of the superficiality of Israeli life?

SH: Well, Israeli society has always been very practical, very goal-oriented. A certain kind of egotism, self-centeredness goes with this—a lack of empathy. The first of the new settlers who came here came voluntarily, like yourself. People tend to forget the difference between this and the postwar, more practical *aliya.* In order to start again in this land, the idealists wanted to forget, to obliterate their past. But when you amputate your past, you pay a price. Part of that is the failure of empathy.

When the massive Eastern *aliya* occurred in the early 1950s,

I was among the few who realized what was happening. I was then serving in the army with special responsibility for a number of transitory immigrant camps. These forced immigrants from Arab countries wanted to stick to their former customs at a time when Israel was committed to our version of the melting-pot theory, which was prevalent as well in the 1950s in America and recognized only by very few as the failure that it was.

There's a story that I once told to an American who lived for some years in Israel; he's now back in the States. He writes articles about us in intellectual journals, and has recently published a book about Israel's failures wherein he utterly misquotes me. No, I shan't mention his name.

What happened was that in one of the immigrant camps under our care the women soldier–teachers, trying to help fashion their girl pupils into Instant Israelis, sat up all of one night at sewing machines shortening the girls' skirts. The next day the fathers of the pupils beat their daughters for wearing the short skirts of prostitutes. This is the sort of uninsightful miscalculation that did happen too frequently, and, as the officer in charge of those teachers, even at the time I tried to point it out. This writer I referred to, by the way, targeted me as one of the well-intentioned soldier–teachers! It makes me furious even to think about.

HC: But at the time, wasn't there real discrimination?

SH: What needs to be said is that we did not ever deliberately discriminate against Oriental Jews. It was a situation of deadlock: one side was frustrated because it was not listened to and its way of life was ignored, the other side frustrated because of the seeming refusal of the newcomers to conform, which was perceived as threatening. Don't forget that we absorbed immigrants at the rate of one hundred per cent over a period of months! One immigrant to one Israeli, a process that simply cannot be done—or, at any rate, done well.

HC: Do you agree with many that this period contains the main source of the Sephardi–Ashkenazi tensions we feel today?

SH: These have been highly exaggerated, even exacerbated, mainly for political reasons. About one-third of all Jewish marriages now taking place in Israel are "mixed"—Sephardi–Ashkenazi—and the rate mounts all the time.

HC: How do you account for the evident increase in polarization between the religious and non-religious sectors in Israel?

SH: Well, for one thing you mentioned that you have a son in a *hesder* yeshiva and that you are dovish, so your crocheted *kippa* is a "good" *kippa*. Many of us, especially here in Jerusalem— which sometimes feels like the frontline of an ongoing war—feel very strongly against the other kind of *kippa* [black, generally worn by the ultra-Orthodox]. Still, though there has been an intensification of tunnel vision, of efforts by fundamentalists to impose rigid constraints on us all, mostly the status quo has been maintained. Nevertheless, the pressure to conform to religious norms is simply unbearable and has led increasingly to acts of violence, the result of which is to divide us each against the other.

HC: How do you account for this burgeoning of religious fanaticism among us Jews?

SH [smiles]: Funny you should ask. I addressed myself to this dilemma in an article in a recent issue of *The Jerusalem Quarterly.* In brief, there are four interrelated ways in which our whole culture has gone off the rails before our very eyes: (one) in the subordination of the rule of law to the way of faith; (two) in the misguided perception of our times as "The End of Days," thereby validating excess as acceptable Jewish behavior; (three) in conferring excessive authority on rabbinic figures; and (four) in the abolition of a sense of sin—which is contrary to the spirit of the Bible. I consider all of these to be deviations from Judaism.

HC: Could you exemplify at least one of these?

SH: Yes, of course. There is an unfortunate wealth of such instances. Not long ago one of our revered rabbis here in Jerusalem, who apparently had carried out every one of the commandments of the Torah save one, decided to achieve perfection by performing it: the *mitzva* [religious duty] of letting the mother-bird go. As you may recall, Deuteronomy 22:6 states that if one happens upon a nest with a mother-bird, it is permitted to take the young, but "thou shalt . . . let the mother-bird go." The intention of this—a limitation upon cruelty—should be clear to anyone with any sense at all.

What did this saintly rabbi do? He set out deliberately to search for a nest with a mother-bird sitting on its young, took the fledglings, and let the mother go. His pupils saw this and followed suit. Soon there occurred a frantic hunt in the hills of Jerusalem for nests containing birds sitting on their young. Finally, the Society for the Protection of Land and Nature intervened for fear that certain species might be destroyed, and the law was brought to bear on the action. This terminated the episode, but it's a graphic example of the miscomprehension and disregard for reality that prevail in certain religious circles. It leads directly to this past week's destruction of Jerusalem bus stops [whose transparent panels were adorned by pulchritudinous models advertising swimsuits] and does not stop short of higher levels of violence.

Do you know, in the month before the Jewish Terror Groups were arrested and indicted, I printed an article, "Messiah or *Knesset* [Parliament]," that predicted the existence of such organizations? Shulamit Aloni read it aloud at the *Knesset*. "If a writer could predict this," she asked, "why couldn't the authorities?" Anyway, such is the present dilemma in this country— Messiah or *Knesset*? The *Knesset* does not—cannot—prevent the coming of the Messiah, if and when this were to come to pass, but the messianic principle now rampant in some Israeli circles absolutely negates the *Knesset*: that is to say, the law, democracy, and ultimately our statehood. In this I consider myself a follower of the Sages who have taught that even the divine voice does not take precedence over the ruling of a duly-appointed high court. The supremacy of the law is surely one of the greatest tenets of Judaism.

HC: What about the daily deepening of the fissure between Jews and Arabs?

SH: It's very serious, though in a way it has led of late to a heightened awareness of the stranger in our midst. But you should really be talking to my husband, Ablouph, about this. He has instituted a pilot program for the Ministry of Education that aims to promote understanding and better Arab–Jewish relations in the schools: a more pluralistic approach in education. This year's special topic in the schools is Pluralism and Democracy. Have your teachers in Yeroham been participating? They really should.

HC: Yes, they have. Nevertheless, the attitude of the youngsters in my children's classes toward Arabs is still disheartening. And local sentiment in favor of *Kach* [anti-Arab political movement led by Rabbi Meir Kahane] seems to be growing.

SH: The collateral side to this polarization is that it's largely a result of the impasse in the peace process. If the process were to continue after the next elections, the sheer weight of reality would overwhelm the rest. According to all polls, the majority of Israelis today are willing to give up territory. Unclear, however, is the translation of this attitude to a choice of political party. But if the peace process stays stalled, we can expect Israel to decline into a less democratic, less pluralistic, more ethnocentric state—very much worse than it is today.

We cannot live for long with the present state of schizophrenia: with democracy on one side of the Green Line and military law on the other; with citizens' rights on one side and no citizens or rights on the other; with one law on one side, a different law on the other. The effect is a breakdown of norms leading inevitably to brutalization. Young people will sooner or later show the effects of this.

HC: What is your personal estimate of Shimon Peres' performance as Prime Minister?

SH: I think he is doing very well indeed. But I am not at all surprised. I have known him for years. Apart from all else, he is a sensitive, genuinely thoughtful, widely-read person. More-over, he maintains an ongoing dialogue with the intellectual community. Now that is real change from, say, Menachem Be-gin—not to mention Golda [Meir]!

HC: And the rotation agreement?

SH: Peres won't be able to avoid it. And then, I regret, the fruit-ful dialogue—*all* fruitful dialogue, both inside Israel and out—will likely cease.

HC: And what then of the peace process?

SH: There won't *be* any process. Nevertheless, the only route to peace at present is via a National Unity government. So it must happen. In a new election, the *Likud* [center-right party] would probably lose seats to the radical, right-wing parties—*Tehiya* and Kahane—America's "gift" to us.

HC: Unlike most Israelis, you are, I believe, quite familiar with Egyptian society.

SH: My husband and I have been to Egypt many times, and I plan again to visit in January. We have many close friends there. It is a highly traditional society, but women have successfully entered many of the professions, like medicine, social work, law, film, and the media.

HC: The very avenues for post-war Jewish success in America.

SH: Exactly.

HC: How do you feel about our so-called "cold peace" with Egypt?

SH: I much prefer this cold peace to a hot war. But let me tell you about the atmosphere in Egypt in May '82. That was a real honeymoon. Everything was open, even euphoric. We had al-ready given back Sinai, and every Egyptian in the street would stop to tell us that Israel was an honorable nation, one that kept its word. Practically all of our friends were making definite plans to visit Israel for congresses, lectures, or simply for pri-vate purposes. There was a joint exhibition of women painters—Egyptian and Israeli—at the biggest hotel in Cairo. Once they knew we were Israelis, waiters and shopkeepers refused to accept our tips. "You are family now," they would say. And you *know* the level of poverty in Egypt where a teacher earns $40 a month. In May of '82, Egypt was a ball!

HC: And then?

SH: And then Israel invaded Lebanon, and everything, everyone stopped—horrified. One of my Egyptian academic friends later wrote to me that watching the Israeli bombing every night on the news, she couldn't face her children who knew, after all, that she had some Israeli friends. But she closed by saying "Still, I think of you and I trust in you completely." When Emil Grunzweig was murdered during a Peace Now demonstration—I am, of course, a Peace Now member—all of our Egyptian friends managed to send cables of condolence. You can scarcely appreciate how complicated it was for them to have gotten together to have it sent!

All in all, I feel that most Egyptians are happy to be at peace with us. There's been, I think, no change in the feelings of the man in the street. Last year we went again, and I lectured in Hebrew to some thirty Egyptian students at the Israeli Academic Center in Cairo. All spoke excellent Hebrew. I recall especially one bright young woman who was doing her doctorate on Maimonides. Next month my husband will lecture at the Center.

HC: Has the recent incident at Ras Burka [locale on the Red Sea coast where a berserk Egyptian soldier machine-gunned a party of Israeli campers] altered anything?

SH: Emotionally? It was a terrible shock. We knew some of the victims. But we must never make the mistake of confusing a criminal act with a national policy. The soldier now stands trial in Egypt. Contrary to a tenet of Islam, the prosecution has demanded the death penalty. [The soldier was eventually convicted and later committed suicide.] We know that many people there are simply, deeply ashamed. As would I be in their place. It will probably be the first topic in all our conversations.

HC: Let me return to one of your stories about which you just might be a shade more responsive than earlier—"Twilight." Its protagonist returns in a compulsive, repetitive dream to her city at the time of the Holocaust. In the end, she gains some insight or respite from pain. The story seems to convey a need for reconciliation with the past or, at least, a need (and means) of surpassing it.

SH: Or a way to come to terms with guilt. Look at the early settlers on the first kibbutzim. They intentionally left their parents far behind. Their children grew up without any grandparents at all. Family simply didn't seem to matter. The goal was the New Man, the New Woman. And then the Holocaust wiped out all of those abandoned parents. It left in its wake a burden of largely unacknowledged guilt.

One of its first kibbutz manifestations, however indirect, was that suddenly *the family* mattered again. There has been the well-known reversal at most kibbutzim allowing children to sleep in the same house as their parents. Bruno Bettelheim superficially alludes to some of this in his book *Children of the Dream.* (Some of us call it *Dreaming About Children.* It is not, I think, a good book.) Today the family exercises, at the expense of the group, a much greater influence than earlier. Even the *metapelot* [parent substitutes] today don't function as comprehensively as they once did. This whole story reflects this guilt-burdened relationship between the generations.

HC: What is your feeling about the current role of women in Israeli society?

SH: For myself, I have always done just what I wanted. I do have a sense that in Israel this is really less of a problem than in the United States. After all, in periods of emergency our women have always carried a heavy responsibility and functioned in most capacities in what still is, in some ways, a pioneer country. That makes it very hard to deny us appropriate roles. Moreover, it springs right from the Jewish family tradition of women serving as breadwinners while their husbands study. I know that Israeli society is famous for being rather macho. But my experience is that any woman who has something to say is listened to.

HC: Well, you certainly are. Your newspaper articles are read by half-a-million people. And you seem to have experienced little difficulty in successfully combining your career with your marriage.

SH: That's not so extraordinary. Here again, Israel may differ from America. Two careers, generally speaking, are a necessity. My husband served in the military and in the defense establishment for thirty years. He now serves on the Board of Directors of the Van Leer Institute. We have two children who have turned out very well, but they would not want me to talk about them.

HC: Have you spent much time in the United States?

SH: Not really. Once I spent a fortnight as scholar-in-residence at Ohio State. I have no original or strong impressions save that the level of intensity of feeling, for some very obvious reasons, seems much lower than here in Israel.

HC: What about the writer's position in Israel? Do you actually make a living at it?

SH: At times I think that writing for the newspapers is an Israeli writer's reserve duty. As you surely know, no Israeli can live on literature alone, simply because this is a small country and the market is limited. It should be said that Israel is a very literate country, and a best seller can sell from 70,000 to 100,000 copies. Nevertheless, authors get paid only a few times a year, and the effect of inflation is to nibble away at our royalties. That's just the way the system works.

I also have a thing about translations. Of course, I recognize that they are necessary, and in Hillel Halkin I know that I have one of the very best of translators. But through no fault of his, we quarrel for hours over my work. English is simply less of a synchronic language than Hebrew.

HC: Some writers claim to ignore their translations.

SH: They may say it, but I don't believe it.

HC: I'm not sure. I'm finding Israeli writers to be an unusually forthright lot. Thank you very much.

SH: Not at all. Look, I even got all my clothes hung out. Now *that's* the way one combines family and career.

Over two years later, it fell my lot to review The Miracle Hater *for the* Post, *which led in turn to a second meeting with Shulamith Hareven in April 1988, five months after the start of the Palestinian uprising.*

HC: It's good to see you again. Didn't I read that you recently won some new award?

SH: Yes. On the occasion of Israel's fortieth Independence Day, eleven women were chosen by the Council of Women's Organizations to be honored for impressive achievement in a ceremony at the *Knesset.* I was among them.

HC: I enjoyed reading *The Miracle Hater* very much. The review should appear any week now. How is it doing in the States?

SH: North Point Press issued it a few months ago. I'm happy to say that it's earning rave reviews in publications like the *Village Voice* and *Publishers Weekly.* Also of interest is that *City of Many Days* will be published later this year in Paris in a French translation.

HC: I know that in recent weeks you have stayed with friends of yours at the Jhabalia refugee camp in the Gaza Strip, and that you've described what you've witnessed in *Yediot Ahronot.* I realize the difficulty of summing up your impressions in brief, but would you try?

SH: In a phrase, we have been badly over-reacting. Look, we have been harassing and humiliating the Arabs for twenty years. Sooner or later, this uprising had to come. Anyone who thinks it was P.L.O.-inspired is out of his mind. In fact, the P.L.O. is trying to catch a free ride on what is happening and for the most part is finding itself impotent.

Instead of applying the techniques of conflict-resolution to solve the problem, we have tried to bulldoze it out of existence. Violence, however, will achieve nothing because the Palestinians really are not "out to get us," and in any case are unable to do so. They are fighting for their identity. As a girl student in Gaza told me, "Please understand that in order to co-exist with you, first we must exist."

HC: And what about Israel's legitimate security needs?

SH: I, for one, would trust the experts. Recently a group of over one hundred reserve generals—the top ones, in fact—have publicized their judgment that giving up territory would not at all be inimical to our security. The spokesman for the generals is General Aharon Yariv, head of the much-respected Institute of Strategic Studies. The group concluded that, contrary to what some may think, staying in the territories would be infinitely more harmful to Israel than would at least a partial withdrawal. This is both for demographic reasons and on account of the need to maintain supremacy of the law. Moreover, having the army engage in police work when it should be preparing for combat situations is definitely harmful to our security. More and more of our soldiers are returning from service on the Bank and Gaza feeling deeply disgusted. This is a mistaken use of the army, and it is definitely weakening us.

You know, I am not a pacifist, Haim. I fought in the War of Independence, and I have covered several wars, including Yom Kippur on the Golan Heights, as a correspondent. But both in the Lebanese War and in these past months of overkill in our reaction to the uprising, we seem to have lost our ability to differentiate between the necessary use of force and plain aggression. For everyone's sake, I hope we regain a proper perspective very soon.

HC: Amen.

Aryeh Liphshitz

Eighty-four and Not at Peace

In his youth a stonemason, Aryeh Liphshitz served for many years
as personal secretary to Henrietta Szold at Youth Aliya and as
editor of its monthly publication. He authored five volumes of
short stories, three books of literary criticism, and numerous es-
says on Israeli life. Into his 80s he still served as Chairman of the
Jerusalem branch of the Israel Writers Association.

It was a rainy afternoon in January 1986. With no difficulty, I
found Liphshitz's apartment next to Jerusalem's Rubin Academy
of Music, just a bit down the street from the official residence of
the President of Israel. Not long before I had written a review of
his short-story collection We Built Jerusalem (Herzl Press), but it
had not yet appeared in print. He graciously greeted and escorted
me into his living room. A short, spry, elderly man whose frame
was still broad and muscular, he evidentally lived alone in the
large apartment. The walls were covered with scores of paintings,
mostly impressionist landscapes and portraits.

Haim Chertok: It's good to get inside from the rain.
Aryeh Liphshitz: Welcome. As you can see, I am an old man
now, but I think you will find that my mind is as alert as ever.
HC: You have quite a collection of paintings.
AL: Yes, I have been a collector for many years. Please sit down.
HC [handing him the March '84 issue of *Jewish Frontier* featuring the interview I had conducted with Aharon Appelfeld]: Our
conversation will probably first appear in a journal like this,
then ultimately, I think, in a collection of interviews I've been
holding with Israeli writers like yourself, Appelfeld, Dan Pagis,
others.
AL [skimming abstractedly through the pages]: I was Appelfeld's
counselor when he was a boy. He first came to Israel with Youth
Aliya after the war. You know I worked for twenty-five years with
Youth Aliya as Henrietta Szold's assistant . . . until her death.
We were very careful to check each child who came to us for any
native talent—musical, artistic, whatever—and often obtained
a stipend so that they could develop it.

HC [smiling]: And how good were you as a talent scout? Did you obtain a stipend for Appelfeld?

AL: You know, I am really not sure. I think he was a late starter.

HC: When did you yourself arrive in Israel?

AL: I came from Cracow in Poland in 1920, and almost immediately I began to work in construction . . . as a common laborer.

HC: You came without your family—completely alone?

AL [smiles]: Oh yes. I had, you see, to make my escape from my father's house. My father and grandfather were both *hachamim* [learned, religious men]. What my father said about Palestine and Zionism was that if God Himself didn't build the Temple, no Temple would be built. As for me, I felt that the soil of Poland was burning under my feet. I knew that I must leave Cracow. It was a city, you know, of great Torah scholars—Rav Katov Sofer, many others. [Pause] So with seven companions I escaped for Palestine. I was eighteen.

HC: I imagine that those first days and months are still intensely vivid?

AL: Oh yes. Can you imagine that it took us three months to get here! In Vienna we were informed that it was simply impossible to proceed. Then we went to the office of JOINT [Joint Distribution Committee, to assist Jewish refugees]. It was just after World War One. They managed to get us as far as Trieste where we signed on as common mariners on a merchant ship. It took us twenty-four days via Yugoslavia, Greece, Egypt, and Italy to reach Haifa. On arrival the authorities sent us immediately— with no military training—to the Upper Galilee to fight. This was one month before the fall of [Joseph] Trumpeldor in the North at Tel Hai [Jewish settlement attacked by Arabs rebelling against French in 1920].

HC: Which "authorities"? Who sent you to fight against whom in Galilee?

AL: Yes, well there was, of course, no Jewish Agency then. It was *Hapoel Hatza'ir* [Young Workers Party]. Everything for us workers came through either *Hapoel Hatza'ir* or *Poale Zion* [Workers of Zion], one little workers' party or the other. We didn't have a united Labor Party yet. I became a construction worker—a mason, a stone-dresser.

HC: And how did you begin your writing?

AL: Prior to coming to Israel, I had done no writing at all. Everything, all of the writing comes from the stones of Jerusalem. A story for me is like the stones for a wall. The lines, the pieces have to fit just so. Anyway, I wrote some short sketches and had the *chutzpah* [colossal nerve] to mail them to Moshe Sharett of the Jewish Agency Executive—then, of course, he was still Moshe Shertok—who had a genuine interest in literary matters. He showed them to Berl Katznelson, the editor at *Davar* [Labor Federation newspaper]. The two of them sent for me to come to Tel Aviv.

As you can well imagine, I, an unknown immigrant laborer, was very agitated, very excited. They asked me to show them my other stories. There were no other stories, but they told me to send them everything I wrote from then on. Till this very day, whatever I write is published first in the literary pages of *Davar.*

HC: How do you account for the sadness, the melancholy that seems to suffuse so many of the stories in the *We Built Jerusalem* collection? Protagonists seem overwhelmed and are often defeated by the tensions and hardships that confront them.

AL: It is sad but real. The truth is that it was very, very hard, too hard for many of the weaker ones. Winter and summer we lived in tents. It was that way for years. But I intended the underlying feeling to dwell not so much on the hardships as on my love for the country. And I mean for the Arabs as well. Two of the stories, "Jum'a and Jamila" and "Under the Horses' Hooves," are about Arabs.

HC: Yes, of course. I noted that for my forthcoming review of the book [*Ariel*, Spring 1986]. Was "Jum'a and Jamila" based on actual experience? It has a premise so fantastic that I thought you

probably didn't invent it, that it must really have been based on
what happened.

AL: Absolutely. For more than a year, while seemingly merely at
work on a construction project, my real work in Trans Jordan
was a secret, a special mission. The three of us who were Jews
never revealed ourselves. We were "Europeans" with no connection to the Jews of the Arabian peninsula or to Israel. The
Jewish Agency, you see, wanted to know what was going on
across the Jordan where Jews were prohibited by the British
from settling.

Till this day I have a connection with, a special feeling for the
Arabs. I speak Arabic fluently. Hebrew and Arabic are really so
similar. They say "our forefather Abu Avrahim." Did you know
that in the Koran it is Ishmael, not Isaac, who is brought by
Abraham to the *Akedah* [Binding of Isaac]?

HC: Yes, I was aware of that. In fact, *were* it Ishmael, that
would help to resolve the problematic matter of Isaac's age at the
time.

AL: I was very interested in visiting the Jews of Arabia, the tribe
called *Yahud Heber.* I rode once for six-and-a-half hours on a
camel to reach an outpost of this tribe. When the Jews on the
peninsula were confronted by Mohammed, over 60,000 were
slaughtered. The remainder stayed and to this day are called
Yahud Heber. Today they are, of course, devout Moslems, with
no memory of their Jewish origins, but they maintain two curious, tell-tale customs: they don't work on Shabbat, and they
don't eat camel meat.

HC: There are, I understand, tribes like that in Afghanistan. It's
curious to think about remnants of our Lost Tribes giving the
Russians such a thumping.

AL: Of course, these *Yahud Heber* perceive not only Abraham
but figures like Sarah and Hagar very differently from us. Many
Arabs still come here to visit with me. Not only my old work-
mates; also their children. Some want to learn Hebrew better.

HC: Your relation to the Arabs is very different from that of several "dovish" Israeli writers I've spoken with. I'm thinking particularly of A. B. Yehoshua. He remarked that, even in bicultural Haifa, though he is acquainted with some Arab actors, he really has no Arab friends.

AL [smiling]: That doesn't surprise me. In contrast to him and many other writers, I have worked with and known the Arabs intimately for most of my lifetime. In fact, would you believe that my best friends back in the 1930s were not our fellow Jews? They were Arabs! And I am talking about my very closest friends. And I have, as I say, close Arab connections to this day.

Let me say something, however, about which it's very hard to convince some well-meaning people, people like A. B. Yehoshua. Even the professors among the Arabs are in some ways almost primitive. For them, the religion of Mohammed is the last word and the only real word. Something that many well-intentioned Jews do not comprehend about the Arabs is that they don't really understand the very concept of compromise. It is not truly part of their vocabulary or mental framework. Probably most of those who are urging peace talks with the Arabs don't know anything about them. It is a dangerous ignorance.

HC: Would you counsel any particular course of action in our present, seemingly endless impasse with the Arabs?

AL: There is really just one solution. [Lengthy pause] It is so simple. [Even longer pause!] The Jews must be here. Still today, after all these years of Israel's independence, only twenty per cent of the world's Jews are physically here. Can you believe it? Twenty per cent! Meanwhile, eighty per cent remain outside waiting for something, perhaps for another Hitler to come. Every country eventually experiences its crises and has its difficulties. When that happens, history again and again has declared that it inevitably turns on its Jews. It's the old but recurrent story of the scapegoat. [Smiles] In this too the Jews were first.

HC: Do you really think that history is all that predictable?

AL: What was the end of my family? Poland! That could serve as a very type of the tragedy of the Jewish people. We are always on the outside. Believe me, it was very, very hard when I came here. But we pioneers *did* something to change our objective conditions. But when the land was ready, the preponderance of Jews still did not come.

The fighting, the squabbling, the endless divisions of our political parties, really don't you see why it continues? Each blames the other for the simple failure of the Jews to come. Because we are still only a very few people here. Do you think that if we were ten million Jews it would be like this? Both from the Jewish and from the Arab point of view, *everything* would be objectively and subjectively different.

HC: You sound so certain?

AL [laughing]: Of many things I have my human doubts, but yes, of this I am certain. I have lived here now for sixty-six years. If only ten million Jews were living here, working here, raising their children here, filling the land with Jewish sweat and lives, all the factionalism, the division, the discord would qualitatively alter. And I include in this the Arabs. Unlike many "theorists," I talk with them. I know. What keeps them so hostile and stubborn is that they are keenly aware that the Jews don't want to come. *They are counting on us!* It makes me so sad.

HC: I can see.

AL: Though my health is good and my mind is sound, I am now an old man of eighty-four. Yet I have little peace. I wake up in the middle of the night, many nights, trying to understand what has happened to this people. My generation suffered and made a revolution for this people. It is impossible not to see it, not to feel it. And yet still the Jews don't come, and still Jews here leave this land. What kind of people is this?

You read my story, "Master of His Fate," about Benjamin Goldwasser. It's a true tale. In the 1920s many Jews actually left Palestine to fight for the Soviet Union, to fight for the idea of brotherhood which they said would also be good for the Jews.

They were all used, exploited, and killed or murdered.

HC: You mentioned that your own family background was religiously observant.

AL: Yes, I was a yeshiva student until I was sixteen. My father didn't allow me to go to an ordinary school.

HC: So the story "Gates of Joy," in which the religious father smiles benevolently at his son who goes off with the secular workers, is something of a fantasy or wish-fulfillment?

AL: Yes, yes, of course. There is a passage in the *Mishnah* [early rabbinic writings] that it was an act of God's charity to the nations of the world to disperse the Jewish people among them. But isn't it enough? Isn't 2,000 years enough of this charity? Anyway, I have my simpler answer. It's not original, but it's so obvious that it fills me with pain: the majority of the Jewish people of the world must be *here*. And they must work. They must be bakers, farmers, lawyers, and—yes—masons.

Three blocks from here, where the Jewish Agency Building now stands, there once stood a labor camp that held three hundred fifty of us boys and girls. We Jews in those days did *all* of the building. Now when they build a huge new synagogue in Jerusalem, the labor is one hundred per cent Arab! And the further irony of it is that it was men like me, men with a strong traditional background, who knew how to make friends with the Arabs.

HC: Have you ever tried proclaiming your "simple solution" among the Jews of the Diaspora?

AL: I once spent two weeks in America. I had been invited to attend a seminar in Mexico, and stopped there en route. Yes, I spoke to many people. One man's response I'll never forget: "The steak in America is thicker than it is in Israel. Why then should I go there?" And this happened not before but *after* Hitler.

People deny it, it is unfashionable, I know, but I tell you that for the Jews, it is exactly in America today as it was for us in Germany. The German Jews used to look down on us Polish

Jews, on us *Ostjuden* [Jews from Eastern Europe]. "We are on top," they would say; "on top of the world of literature, of finance, of the professions. We are Deutsch." It has ever been the same for us Jews in other countries, among other cultures. *This* is the source of the pain that runs all through my book, through all of my books.

HC: Is *We Built Jerusalem* your first book to appear in English?

Al: Yes. I was approached by Mishcha Louvish, the well-known translator. He asked if I would like a selection of my stories to appear in English. I made my choice—it is only a very small selection of my work—and then he made all the arrangements. Some of my untranslated stories deal with the early days in Palestine, others with my father and grandfather and the pain of life in *galut.*

HC [looking at some photos on the wall]: This is your family?

AL: Yes, my son is an agricultural expert. He recently attended a conference in Asia. I have six grandchildren and two great-grandchildren. But my wife died seven years ago, and I now live here alone.

HC: You are still, I understand, Chairman of the Jerusalem branch of the Hebrew Writers Association. What function does that organization serve?

AL: Yes, it is ten years now. [Smiles] I would like to retire. They won't let me. We are members of PEN international, and not long ago we hosted a Congress of PEN in Jerusalem. That took a lot of work. Every two years there is a conference of the Central Committee of the Israel Writers Association. Simply enough, we help with the special needs and problems of the Hebrew writer. We try to help writers get their books published.

At present, the situation for new writers in Israel is not very good. We also help young writers who do not yet write in Hebrew. For example, there's Israel Zarchis, a talented young man who writes in Polish. Some young writers, though, have crazy ideas. One young poet, a *Hashomer Hatza'ir kibbutznik*—don't mention his name!—compares the Jews to the Nazis. He writes poems that say that we eat our *matzot* with the blood of Lebanese. Terrible things. [Smiles] But would you like something to eat and drink? Come! [We moved to the kitchen table, to tea and cookies.] I am, by the way, a vegetarian.

HC: What is your current literary project?

AL: I am glad you asked. I am deeply engrossed in preparing a two-volume work on how Hebrew literature developed from its origins in the nineteenth century. I want to show the younger generation from where they come. I deal with figures like Hayim Hazaz [b. 1898] and Shai Agnon, trying to show that they, as opposed to many others, actually created new things. Of course I also, from time to time, write my stories. My last book was for young people: *Till They Came Home.* It's about Israel and the Diaspora. This is ever the burning problem at my heart.

HC: Will you deal in your new book with Brenner?

AL: Yes, of course. I knew Joseph Hayyim Brenner; in fact, I consider myself his disciple. We met in 1920 at the first convention of *Histadrut* [unified labor federation]. We younger workers demanded then that there be one, united *Histadrut,* one workers' organization instead of several organizations affiliated to political parties. Between the sessions Brenner spoke only to us youngsters. I knew that his first book had been first published in my native Cracow, three streets, in fact, from my very own house. Brenner was pessimistic and very sad about the Jewish people: "They want the West," he said. "They reject our history. But," he continued, "when I see you young people, I am heartened. There will yet be something."

I am also a follower of Rav Avraham Kook [1865–1935], the former Chief Rabbi of Israel, who was chastised by the ultrareligious elements of his day for bothering to talk with us laborers. He would tell them that we youngsters were performing the highest *mitzva* possible, the settling of the Land of Israel. As for the other *mitzvot,* he told them that in God's good time, he was confident we would move on to them. Meanwhile, he strongly supported us. This was in 1925 at the opening of Hebrew University, a project I worked on for two years as a construction worker.

[Reflective pause] You know, Haim, I did something in this country. Even outside of this country. Yet though I am eighty-four, I am not quiet, and I am not at peace. I simply cannot accept or understand how, especially after the Holocaust, so many Jewish people can stay away from our land.

Outside it was raining harder. Nevertheless, Liphshitz accompanied me with an umbrella past the Rubin Academy to Auster Square, one of the loveliest in Jerusalem.

AL: All this was stone and rock when I first came here. We youngsters lived for four years right here, in the rain and snow, in tents.

Come and visit me again, with your wife, Haim, whenever you want.

HC: Thank you. You may count upon it.

But I was mistaken. We were never to talk again. Suffering from a number of internal disorders, Aryeh Liphshitz was admitted several months later to Jerusalem's Share Tzedek Hospital where he languished until his death on August 6, 1986.

Later Aloma Halter, Associate Editor at Ariel, *told me that about a week before his passing she visited Liphshitz at the hospital and handed him my review of* We Built Jerusalem [Ariel, *Spring 1986*].

"He read it, and he showed it proudly to the people at his bedside. For half-an-hour, anyway, his face brightened into a smile, and he forgot his illness," she reported.

Benjamin Tammuz

World's Number Two Canaanite

*Well-known, widely-translated novelist Benjamin Tammuz lives
on a quiet street of apartment buildings that parallels Dizengoff
Street, Tel Aviv's brassiest, broadest way. Born in Russia in 1919,
vigorous-looking, eyes deep-set, he sports a prominent, bushy
mustache.*

*It was early on an afternoon in February of 1986. His airy flat
was situated on the very top floor of the apartment building; apparently, he lived alone. On the balcony a leafy row of potted
plants throve. We sat at a table in the dining area.*

Haim Chertok: Climbing up to your apartment must keep you in
good shape, Mr. Tammuz.
Benjamin Tammuz: I am feeling fit. The stairs are not so very
much: just fifty steps altogether. By the way, I pronounce my
name Támmuz; it's spelled with two m's to maintain that stress
on the first syllable. Are you hungry from your long journey from
Yeroham? Would you like a sandwich?
HC [handing him a back number of the *Jewish Frontier* which he
rapidly skimmed]: No, thank you. Just a cup at tea would be
nice. This is the periodical in which our conversation will eventually appear.
BT: Here's a poem by Robert Friend. I know him. [Loud noise
from the adjacent room distracted us.]
HC: You have a tenant?
BT [laughing]: No, it's just a carpenter who's doing some re-
modeling work. He's now finishing up for the day and will be
gone in a few minutes. I'll be back in a minute. [He disappeared
for a moment into the kitchen, reappearing with a dish of halvah
and dates and two cups of tea.] Products of the Land of Israel.
HC: Actually, I took the bus to get here today not from Yeroham
but from Jerusalem, reversing the journey that Rehavya Abramson took in my favorite of your stories—"Angioxyl, A Rare
Cure." It feels strange for me to walk around in Tel Aviv, something like traveling in a foreign country. Almost everyone I know

away from the Negev seems to live in Jerusalem. Do you really enjoy living in the very heart of Tel Aviv?

BT: Well, since my parents brought me to Palestine from Russia at the age of five, I have been an urban person almost all of my life. I lived for a year in Paris. Ten years in England—five in London, five in Oxford—that was very fine. I don't think about it much; I suppose I'm just used to it.

HC: Might you run through the books you have written to date?

BT: It's not all that hard. Let me see. There are now eight novels, six collections of short stories, and seven books for children.

HC: And in English? You may recall that I reviewed the collection featuring "Angioxyl" in the [*Jerusalem*] *Post* a few years ago when it was published in paperback in translation.

BT [laughing]: Of course, I recall. That was the review that showed how much you liked my book by contrasting it to that novel by that married couple who live on a kibbutz . . .

HC: . . . The Seneds.

BT: . . . Yes, the Seneds . . . which you hated. That was wicked of you.

HC: I suppose that you're right, but it was just chance that the two translations from Hebrew came my way at the same time. It's common practice to . . .

BT: . . .Oh, I know that. I was a newspaper literary editor for many years. And I'm glad that I wrote the book that you liked. It's just that when I read that review, I felt sorry for them. Though I was innocent, they were scourged by my book. It's not really your fault, but still, there was something unfair in it.

HC: Which of your other books have appeared in English translation?

BT: Well, there's *Castle in Spain* for Bobbs-Merrill in the States, Gollancz in England; *Requiem for Naaman* for New American Library; *Minotaur* also for N.A.L.

HC: Yes, I've heard about it, but I haven't read it yet.

BT: It was named the best novel of 1982 by Graham Greene in

The Observer, and has appeared in French as well. Then *The Orchard* was put out by the Copper Beech Press, a small publisher in Providence, Rhode Island.

HC: Copper Beech Press! Why, you must know Edwin Honig at Brown University. That press is his hobbyhorse. He's an old, good friend, a very fine poet, and a former professor of mine.

BT: Oh yes? I met him once here in Israel. A very nice, gentle man.

HC: Have you been writing all your life?

BT: Since the age of twenty-eight. Before that I was a sculptor. I studied in Paris. Then I won a competition with a piece called "Monument to a Bird." Perhaps you've seen it on display in Jerusalem at the Israel Museum? After that I gave up sculpture to work at writing. It was as if I had completed something and needed to move on to something else.

HC: Like many Israeli writers, you seem to be very prolific. In fact, it's something of a mystery to me. Israeli writers can't make a living exclusively from writing, but they seem to produce at least as much as writers in the Diaspora.

BT: That's true. Though you know that Agnon and Hayim Hazaz both received stipends from organizations, so they were more or less financially free. And, of course, there is one Israeli who makes real money from his writing—[humorist Ephraim] Kishon [b. 1924, living in Switzerland]—if you want to call his work "writing." [Laughs] I suppose that what you could fairly conclude is that most of us writers are crooks. We neglect our paying jobs to sneak in our real work.

But you know I have heard, though it's just literary gossip, that Amos Oz, were he not a member of a kibbutz, could survive nicely on his earnings. His novels must now bring in around $20,000 a year, which is very, very good. But he is unique. The rest of us have to be a little crooked to get it all in.

HC: Would you comment on your close involvement with the literary—intellectual secularist movement, the Canaanites?

BT: Ah! You are sitting across from the Number Two Canaanite in the world. I first met Yonaton Ratosh [b. 1908] in 1939. Almost at once I felt strongly attracted to his idea that we Jews here in Israel should disconnect ourselves from the 2,000 years of dismal Diaspora and its rabbinic culture. Rather, he argued, we should look further back into our roots and identify with a Canaanite past. That would have provided a sounder self-image for our reconstituted people. I became Ratosh's disciple; I did for him, in fact, what Saint Paul did for Jesus. And I believe that we made a major impact, but you know, there weren't really ever more than a small band of a dozen of us. All of us Canaanites were caught and collected by me!

But then in 1950 an odd thing happened. When finally I went abroad, to the despised Diaspora itself, I suddenly came to realize that the Jews of Paris were also my brethren. That put a damper on my Canaanitism.

HC: You found that the ideology had certain limitations.

BT [laughing]: True, but years later, when I was assigned to London as Cultural Attaché to the Israeli Embassy, I again met up with Diaspora Jews. That time it was profoundly different. How rotten a disappointment it was! But it was too late. I was already too conversant with Judaism and had identified myself as one of the lepers.

You know, I once published a story about a second encounter with the angel. You remember when Jacob encountered the angel at the ford of the Jabbok and defeated him at all-night wrestling? That won him the title "Israel" and the renewal of the promise of Abraham to inherit the land. Have you heard of Simone Weil [1909–1943], not the present French Minister of Culture or whatever she is, but another French Jewess named Simone who in the Forties, on the verge of converting to Catholicism, held back out of loyalty to the Jewish people during the Holocaust?

HC: Like Henri Bergson. Yes, I know who you mean. She wasn't the first Jew who felt drawn to Saint Theresa.

BT: Yes, that's the one. She didn't survive the war. Anyway she once wrote that it is an awful thing to win a battle with a God. I agree with her. The time has long passed when we should hang on to the exclusive title of Chosen People. We should return the diploma. Who really needs this burden any more? What endless trouble it has brought us! I think second meetings are the most meaningful. A return engagement with that angel is long overdue. We should be wise and clever enough this time to throw the match.

You should know, I am actually a sort of a "Christian"—with the quotes, of course. I really like that good Jew, Jesus Christ, who never intended anything of what followed in his wake. Not that crazy bastard Paul, of course. Paul was a disaster. Did you know that he went all the way to Georgia? When he came back, James blamed him for preaching to the *goyim* [non-Jews]. Paul had missed, you see, the whole point. Jesus came to preach to us Jews, not to the *goyim*. He was always meant for the Jews.

HC: Like India was meant for Columbus? So Paul ended up with the Indians, and we Jewish Hindus couldn't care less. Actually, good intentions matter more, I think, for Christians than for Jews. Doesn't what actually happened with Christianity—its blood-filled history—say more than a time-stranded figure named Jesus?

BT: It could be. Let me tell you something about my latest book, *The Inn of Jeremiah.* [He gestured toward my *kippah.*] You probably wouldn't much like it. It is a description of the near future when the Temple has been rebuilt, and instead of a *Knesset,* we have a reconstituted Sanhedrin running our lives. It is a monstrosity. Really, it is a nasty book, but it's one of my favorites of those I've written. It simply overflows with Judaism—and all based on *halacha* [Jewish religious law]. Like hitting below the belt! The epigraph about the Sanhedrin is taken from *Midrash Rabbah* [classic of rabbinic homilies and stories]. You know, one of my favorite people was Rav Avraham Kook, the former Chief Rabbi of the country. Some of my books have been best sellers and created scandals, but my works are forbidden, I've been told, in the *yeshivot*. Someone at Yeshivat Mercaz Harav told me that I was proscribed. Too much explicit sex, perhaps. I don't know. Apparently they don't like to read about such things in the *yeshivot*.

HC: Not exactly. My older son studies at a *hesder* yeshiva—Har Etzion. He just has lots to read in limited time. But he allots himself about an hour a day for "general reading." I am fairly certain that there, at least, no books are proscribed as such.

Your earlier novel that New American Library published, *Requiem for Naaman*, has, at least for the American reader, some resemblances with Faulkner: the sense of doom that strikes down the first mother Bella-Yaffe, the primal flaw to Abramson's whole enterprise (in this case, Zionism). Might you more explicitly identify what you perceive as that flaw or sin which corresponds to slavery for Faulkner?

BT: I suppose, but it's almost vulgar to be talking about these things. Let me just say that fulfilling an ideal is always a disappointment. Ideals should never be attained. The more you fulfill them, the more gets spilled and lost. Oscar Wilde, that supreme artist of *galut*, said it best: It is a terrible thing in life never to attain your goal; the only worse thing is to achieve it. Aspiration is more than fulfillment. Here, with the establishment of the State of Israel, a disaster has occurred. We "achieved" it! You see, that Jew Jesus had it right about kingdoms on earth and in heaven: we humans really are made of rotten stuff.

HC: You stayed on in England for fully ten years. I assume that you must have seriously contemplated remaining there.

BT: Yes, but here I am! Listen: Jews live here, they live there. It happens, it is personal, and it is life.

HC: But for the survival of the Jewish people, are such matters strictly "personal," as you put it, or merely neutral facts?

BT: Very simply, if human beings suffer, *that*'s a disaster. But where is the pain if a Jew marries a non-Jew? And what really is the difference if there are twenty million Jews in the world or fifteen million or ten?

HC: Many would differ with you about that.

BT: Perhaps. But it hardly matters how many there are in England or anywhere else. They won't want to come to Israel. Never really did! If Jews are here now, it is mainly out of desperation or economic necessity, as was the case with my father from Russia. Still, maybe it is God who suffers. [Pause] Though I don't know anything at all about God, I consider myself a religious human being.

HC: What were your actual duties as Israel's Cultural Attaché in London for five years?

BT: I asked the Foreign Office about that before I left. They told me to do what I wanted. Actually, I think that I accomplished quite a bit. I compiled for them a selection of contemporary Israeli literature, one of the first published in English. Also, I helped to initiate Hebrew Studies at universities in London, Glasgow, Cambridge, and Manchester. Of course, there were always lots of talks and speeches.

HC: And British Jewry?

BT: London's Jews are a real disaster. All they care about is being more British than the British and making money. At least you in America have some Jewish institutions and men of knowledge: Yeshiva University, the Jewish Theological Seminary in New York. In England, the Jews make money. That's it!

HC: Have you never in your life felt any inclination toward traditional Judaism?

BT: Not really. Once in the late 1930s, my wife and I tried lighting candles and reciting *kiddush* [blessing over wine] on Friday nights. We did it for the children, but our two boys only stared at us as though we had gone quite mad. "Why are you doing this?," they asked. We told them honestly that we were doing it for them. Well, it was a joke. *They* didn't want or need any of that. The *mitzvot* are, I think, simply rabbinic inventions, like works of art.

HC: For the sake of argument, assume that you are correct. Still, have they not taken on for us as Jews an independent value, at the very least as an accessible means of identifying both horizontally in space and vertically in time with the Jewish people?

BT: Yes, I admit that you have a point there.

HC: You spent your second period of five years in England at Oxford?

BT: Yes, I was a visiting writer and lecturer at the university. It was most pleasant.

HC: You have had a lengthy career as a journalist as well, am I right?

BT: Oh, yes. I wrote a satirical column, *Uzi* [short for Uziel, a name], back in the 1940s in *Ha'aretz* [highly respected daily]. It was one of the most popular columns in the country. Once, when Moshe Sharett—you are related to him, are you not?—didn't grant me the appointment as Cultural Attaché when I had expected it, I demanded and was granted an interview with him. (The reason, by the way, was that I had been a member of IZL [revisionist underground organization].) I was about thirty. When he saw me he whispered aloud to a nearby aide in Russian that he had thought from the tone of *Uzi* that I was only eighteen or twenty. I told him not to whisper secrets in Russian, that my Russian was better than his—and it was. We spoke for over an hour. He was charming and attentive . . . but he did not contact me later as he'd promised.

Many years later, after I returned from my decade in England, I served as Cultural Editor at *Ha'aretz*. I wrote about literature, painting, sculpture, everything. But I retired on an early pension in 1978.

HC: Do you miss it?

BT [laughing]: On the contrary, I wanted very badly to get out of it. Finally I figured out a very simple way to do it.

HC: Yes?

BT: No, I cannot tell you about it, but really, it is very simple. Anyone with any brains at all could do it. And since my freedom in 1978, I have produced perhaps half of all my books.

HC: You seem to be getting, with the passing years, increasingly prolific. Among classic American writers—I'm thinking of Melville, Hemingway, Hart Crane, among others—the governing romantic myth is that writers feel compelled to keep topping the younger competition, or else themselves, and often deplete their stock of talent by writing themselves out.

BT: Oh, writing is a lust like eating, sex, or contemplating beauty. I have to write, and I enjoy writing sensually. Sometimes, I even just write lists. Really, it is my greatest joy. The results are, in a way, quite secondary. I enjoy doing it. I have to do it. If I couldn't write, I would be miserable. I plan and hope to keep on with my writing till the very end, even if what I write is worthless.

HC: What are you writing just now?

BT: Actually, I'm a little frightened of it. It is based on a concept that, as far as I know, has never before been tried. I think it will be a many-sided work and a true one. It is an autobiography of the Jewish people since the sixth century—1,350 years of autobiography. The chapters are, in reality, short stories. There are many protagonists, in all one hundred twenty chapters and situations. Moreover, the entire book consists of documents: letters, wills, diaries, etc. I call it *Charmian and the Nightingale.* Yes, that will probably be the final title.

HC: How do you feel about this present moment in Jewish and Israeli history?

BT: I feel very rotten. Really. I have been here since 1924. Can you guess what I think were our best days? They were the ones when we were fighting the British. Since 1948 it's been a downhill slide. [Laughing] I wish we had the British here again. I loved them!

Since '48, when we opened the gates, what have we discovered? The Law of Return—such a foolish business; if it weren't so irrelevant, it should be revoked—set the seal to our abnormalcy. What country says that any of its people who come can automatically become citizens! As I have said, Jews in substantial numbers have never really wanted to come here. Look at your town of Yeroham: it is filled with Moroccan Jews, but not the good or cultured or intelligent ones. *They* all went to France. And on Israel they dumped the Casbah.

HC: That's a bit glib, I think. There are all sorts of Moroccans in Yeroham—and in France as well.

BT: Herzl thought, you know, that Israel would be a haven only for the most miserable Jews. And he also thought that the Arabs would be overjoyed to have them come. What nonsense! But he was really only a fellow journalist like me with an impressive black beard. The only one of that founding generation who really understood the situation was Ahad Ha'am [Asher Ginsberg, 1856–1927]. He wrote that Zionism, that *our* movement, would create the Arab counter-movement. He had it exactly right.

HC: And what of Israel and the Arabs today?

BT: Oh, I may be a former I.Z.L., but I am now a super-dove. We should, of course, be talking with them. After all, we have tried everything else. Every year the 120,000,000 Arabs get stronger and more sophisticated. I don't see how we can continue to cope. We should do something soon. Unfortunately, Shimon Peres is above all a politician, good at pleasing many factions. He lacks the imagination and the power really to make peace. But it is Begin I am most angry with. He was the one who introduced novelties and *Likud* nonentities like Pesach Grupper and David Levy into the Cabinet. Last week Levy was consulting with some nephew of Baba Sali [mystic Moroccan wonder-rabbi] on matters of national policy! And he is a minister in the government! We are going back to African tribal primitivism!

HC: On Grupper and Levy, we can close in full agreement.

Thank you very much indeed. But before my return trip to the Casbah, just one final question. If you had to name only one, which of the younger Israeli writers do you particularly enjoy to read or do you think shows the greatest promise?

BT: That's a difficult question. Israel possesses no shortage of young, talented writers. If I had to name just one, however, it would be Yehoshua Kenaz. He has a wonderful style, a real way with a Hebrew sentence. He lives not far from here. I'll write down his number for you.

HC: Thank you.

BT [moving to bookshelves]: But wait a moment more, and, if I can just find it, I'll lend you a copy of *Minotaur.* Here it is. Take a copy of *Requiem for Naaman* also. But you'll have to be sure to return them. They're the only ones I have left. Next week I'll be leaving for England for a few months. A family visit. You can leave the books in the electricity box in the hallway, after you've finished with them, on some future trip to Tel Aviv. I'll alert my father-in-law to check for them.

HC: Thank you very much indeed. They shall be returned without fail. And have a good trip!

Over a year later I was talking with Yael Medini about the forthcoming publication of her collection of short stories. There had been some delay. "There always is," I consoled. What was the cause?

"An original one," she commented. "After many years of marriage, my publisher's editor's wife has left him. He's such a kind man. I think you mentioned once that you met with the third party—the writer Benjamin Tammuz."

I thought then of what Aharon Appelfeld had said that afternoon in 1983 at the Café Atara. Over the course of time, everyone in Israel who writes gets close to everyone else.

Asenath Petrie

Lover of Jerusalem

It was a spring-like day in March of 1986. At precisely 12:30
P.M., on the terrace overlooking the gardens at Anna Ticho Café
in downtown Jerusalem, poet–scientist Asenath Petrie appeared
wearing a wide-brimmed velour hat and thin raincoat. Earlier I
had reviewed her moving collection of poems, The Lasting Joy
That Is Jerusalem, *and I had become familiar with her distinc-*
tive, British-accented voice by phone. She is tall, angular, per-
haps a bit gaunt, past middle years, and possesses a luminous
smile and commanding presence. Characteristically, she pauses
long between sentences, as if looking back, retrieving an impres-
sion from the past.

We seated ourselves inside what at first was a room to ourselves.
Over the course of the following hour, it gradually filled with
diners.

Haim Chertok: It's very good finally to meet up with you. I had
contrived a mental image of your appearance from your telephone voice. I was, in fact, reasonably close.

Asenath Petrie: Ever since I read your appreciative but search-
ing review of *The Lasting Joy That Is Jerusalem* in *Ariel*, I also
have been looking forward to our meeting. [Pause] I was with
Anna Ticho [1894–1980] often toward the end of her life at the
time when her friend Helen Kagan died. [She indicated the direction, where, a short distance from where we sat, pioneer phy-
sician Kagan had lived.] Anna Ticho had a special way of seeing
things. She lost one eye, but was reluctant to have a cataract
removed from the other. Her husband was a justly famous eye
doctor.

She would have liked the fine transformation they have made
of her home into a museum for her paintings. She was a lovely
lady, extraordinarily gifted. Her burial was at Purim [late winter
Jewish festival] when the snow was still surprisingly deep. But
what do you want to hear about?

HC: In brief, yourself.

AP: You cannot understand me and how I write without knowing about my father. Let me tell you in my own way.

HC: I wouldn't ask for more.

AP: When I was six, my father came to Jerusalem, and I joined him with the rest of the family for six months. He was Rabbi Victor Schonfeld of London. With Rabbi Yisrael Ya'akov Yoffe, he had been co-founder of the Mizrachi Organization [Religious Zionist Movement] in the then still-extensive British Empire. In 1920, at the Mizrachi World Conference in Amsterdam, he was appointed head of the Orthodox Mizrachi School System in the Holy Land. He proceeded to establish new schools and regularized the whole Orthodox educational system throughout the country. He also strove to bring about unity between the factions in the Orthodox camp. [Lengthy hesitation] Then, when despite his unswerving love for this country he saw that certain decisions were putting his basic educational aims in jeopardy, he resigned.

HC: And your mother?

AP: Yes, I have to add a glimpse of our remarkable mother. Undoubtedly the close, complementary relationship of that couple communicated its strength to the whole family. They happened to be, by any aesthetic standard, two outstandingly handsome people of completely different personality. They fitted each other's needs admirably.

It must have strongly affected our mother that she lost her own mother when she was twelve and had younger children for whom to care. It served as a dress rehearsal for when she would be widowed at age thirty-nine with seven children, the oldest nineteen and the youngest just two. She herself had been nineteen and married for just one year when her first child had been born. During those twenty years she enjoyed at the side of the wonderful personality of our father, she grew immeasurably. Self-educated, remarkably intelligent, she had almost excessive energy and an indomitable will. Undoubtedly, her preoccupation with maintaining the institutions her husband had started, with the school at the forefront, influenced the manner in which we children accepted responsibility for each other. Despite extraordinary differences in personality, a feeling of cohesion prevailed. Nevertheless, in later years, perceptive friends said it was unbelievable that we came from the same nursery.

HC: When did you start your work?

AP: My father introduced me to my first private pupil. I often "invested" my money in second-hand books. Pressing my face long and often against the greengrocer's window to get a good view, there was always something of a struggle not to waste some of it on bananas.

The books were shared with my brother Akiba. We read poetry out loud to each other and at times with Beaty Ginsberg, a loyal family friend. Akiba's outstanding work as an economist and writer—he was to become Sir Akiba Andrew—and his unfailing helpfulness and understanding through his sadly short life, contributed immensely to what I have been able to accomplish.

HC: Perhaps we are anticipating. What about your own formal schooling?

AP: I was the only girl, a middle child. As there was not yet a Jewish school for me to attend, we agreed on a Quaker school. It is difficult to convey the pride I felt in my father as he sat with my headmistress-to-be. It didn't occur to me that the world could contain a more wonderful human being. This made me feel a special responsibility not to let him down, not to fall below what was expected of me, since I realized from where I came.

I was needed both for help in the house and to teach in the Jewish school my father had founded in 1929, the year before he died. I started teaching the school's first class in biology even before I had earned my own degree. Except for one girl who should have succeeded, they all passed matriculation. (With that one girl, unfortunately I didn't yet know the ropes well enough to inquire if there had been an error, which I suspected had occurred.) We acted out our biology lessons. On annual Prize Day, the red and white cells, as in a traditional Chinese production, introduced themselves as a prelude to the action.

There wasn't enough money to send me to study at university, but one of my teachers, a lady named Beatrice Griffiths, declared after my father's death, "You are going to university even if I have to pay for you myself." She did, in fact, pay my way for the first year, after which I obtained aid from the university. [We both briefly left to wash hands ritually in order to say the blessing over bread; then we both ordered the vegetable soup.]

HC: Where did you obtain your first degree?

AP: It was at University College, London. A second teacher, Miss Dorothy English, provided money for books. Save for my father, who had a doctorate, I was the first in my family to go to university. At that time it was frowned upon in the Pressburg [Bratislava, Czechoslovakia] Yeshiva circle. [Suddenly looking up] You know, the great Rabbi Avraham Kook had a house just down the road from here. In his memorial address about my father, Rav Kook declared that the knowledge my father had acquired at university made him revere the Almighty all the more.

HC: Such sentiments would mark him as a radical today. And after university?

AP: You've heard of Oswald Mosley and the British Union of Fascists in the East End of London? At the time, it was very powerful. I was serving there as Director of a Settlement House—Bethnal Green Community Center. It was a dangerous place. I mean, there were fights in the streets with flying bottles. It was closed during the war—because of the war, that is. The authorities who planned the closure asked that I take part in the evacuation of children from dangerous areas. That's how I got so involved in the removal of Jewish children from London to Bedfordshire, to a place called Stotfold. I was responsible for over two hundred Jewish children from the ages of four to seventeen.

I suppose I had acquired a great deal of experience with children even before the settlement house. Most of the youngsters were refugees. Many had been helped to escape from the Holocaust through the efforts of my late brother, Rabbi Solomon Schonfeld.

It was difficult not only for us but also for our English village hosts. Some of them were models of tolerance, but with others I had to do battle on the children's behalf. I was once told, for example, "even our enemy Hitler would not put up with them, and yet we are asked to do so."

HC: And may I ask your age at the time?

AP: How old was I? [Smiles] I was then twenty-four, so you can figure out my age from that. In all our twelve months there, we had received only one visit from the neighboring school center. I had one very helpful assistant—Polly Elton—as well as my perceptive brother David, then aged seventeen. What was important was that here, in an extension of the school founded by our father, we were helping to give to these children a feeling of being safe, loved, and approved of, while they were learning to live in a new country.

HC: So during the Blitz you lived and worked outside of London?

AP: Not really. After one year two schools were combined, and I was able to return to London where I worked on related problems with the Jewish Board of Deputies.

One night, while we were pursuing our aim of getting as many of the aged and the mothers with young children out of the Underground shelters and into Jewish homes we had set up for them outside London, Jane Leverson, who was my companion on that occasion, arranged for us to spend that night at her uncle's apartment off Baker Street. What we witnessed from his roof was much of London seemingly engulfed in a sheet of flame.

HC: Do you suppose the ghosts of Holmes and Watson also bore witness?

AP [smiling]: Something I haven't thought of in a long while comes to mind. Earlier that evening, we had had to change trains and walk from one station to another. The streets were almost deserted. Just ahead of us, however, walked a single man. We were both greatly impressed by his unswerving path and erect carriage while the "doodlebugs" were crashing all around. On our arrival, we both complimented him. He put his hand to his ear and asked us to repeat what we had said. Only after further unsuccessful attempts did we realize the degree of his insulation from the din of the exploding incendiaries on that extraordinarily active night during the height of the Blitz.

HC: Images of the Holocaust suffuse much of your poetry. When did your personal connection with the Holocaust become intimate?

AP: I became involved with an independent group of committed, outstanding people who conceived a program to help with concentration-camp victims after the war. We founded relief units which went into the camps. I went to Bergen–Belsen before they cleaned it up. As I wrote later, "at our first encounter, those who outlived that death-camp were still pent up in its corpse." Later in Palestine I witnessed how the British were interning Jewish escapees at Atlit near Haifa. Although the tents in which they lived were stuck in thick mud, they, at least, had arrived home.

The Chairman of that Jewish Committee for Relief Abroad was Dr. Redcliffe Salaman, F.R.S. He became almost a substitute father to me. A remarkable scientist, he had served during World War One as a medical officer in the first Jewish Brigade after 2,000 years. The Jewish Publication Society has published his wife Nina's translation of Yehuda Halevi. The children of Redcliffe and Nina Salaman gave me the Shabbos candlesticks that I use to this day. It was Redcliffe who introduced me to the Cultural Attaché from Israel.

HC: But before Israel came your remarkable professional career.

AP: Yes. Well, I worked in a military hospital in London which was the Neurosis Center for all the Allied Forces. I was a researcher on aspects of mental malfunctioning. I was, in fact, a founding member of the Department. My financial support came from the United States: I was a Rockefeller Fellow. Then, in 1951–52 it was, I received a Fulbright Grant to lecture in the United States.

My Fulbright effectively opened up the U.S.A. and Canada to me. To my amazement, I discovered myself lecturing on my findings about brain function at major hospitals and medical schools all over North America. The Rockefeller Foundation supported my next project as well, and thereafter I served as its Director at the Institute of Psychiatry attached to the Maudesley Hospital in London. Doing my field work as a member of a medical team at Allied Forces Hospital, I received my doctorate in a cross-disciplinary field: neuro-pathological aspects of brain function and the techniques for treating malfunction.

From the States continued to come a series of grants: the National Institute of Health, the Lasker Fund, etc. In 1957, Harvard University suggested that I join its staff. Since it was the source of my funding, it just made sense to make my base in the U.S. [Longer than usual pause.] Prizes came—what the world values. I was invited to the White House, appeared more than once on the *Today* Program. The University of Chicago Press was generous with a lovely edition of my *Individuality in Pain and Suffering*. They brought it out again in paperback, and arranged for a Paris publisher to bring out a French edition.

HC: It sounds as though Israel might well have remained on the periphery of your life.

AP: True, but it was not to be. In fact, the most significant turn in my life occurred during the Yom Kippur War, in 1973. I had previously been in Israel as a Lecturer at the Weizmann Institute and at Hadassah Hospital. Living here, however, decisively affected my values, my direction, my priorities, my life.

From my Jerusalem home, I enjoy a view of a valley that leads straight to the sea. Did you know that until the Yom Kippur War I had never written a single line of poetry?

HC: No, I didn't. Do you sense any conflict between the scientific and poetic sides of your personality?

AP [smiling]: Not that I am aware. In any event, they have blended happily in this unique city. When she was in Jerusalem, Marie Syrkin read my poems and said she wanted to have them. She proceeded to publish three of them in *Midstream.* Some were later translated into Hebrew and other languages. You have published in *Midstream,* haven't you? Also I think in *Commentary* and the *Jewish Frontier?*

HC [nodding]: What have you mainly been up to since coming on *aliya?*

AP: Since arriving in Jerusalem in 1973, I have been blessed not only with wonderful new friends of outstanding loyalty, but the many threads of my life have come together. Friends from the past keep arriving. For a time I worked as a consultant at Hadassah Hospital and elsewhere. I lead a rich life in Israel.

I feel now that I have found a new voice in poetry. Please tell me, what did you mean in your review of *The Lasting Joy That Is Jerusalem* that some of the poems go on too long?

HC: If I recall rightly, I was referring to your tendency to explain your intentions within the poem instead of trusting the reader to understand on his own.

AP: So you think that I should have greater trust in the reader? Thank you.

HC: It is obvious that you love this country and this people. What is your reaction to the severe divisions that sometimes seem to be tearing Israel apart these days?

AP [lengthy, reflective pause]: When Israel was united, it didn't matter how many of us were observant or non-observant. Israel survived on this ground. Today, however, building bridges between seemingly divided groups is of crucial importance. Relatively recently I noticed a passage in our morning prayers,

". . . who forms light and darkness, makes peace and creates everything." First He makes peace between seeming irreconcilables, and then He creates all the other apparent opposites. Nothing *we* are confronted with is as opposed as light and darkness. What we must encourage are all efforts toward their reconciliation. Most of us are aware of the destiny of our people in this land. Because what we have in common is so much greater than our divisions, I feel we should be strengthening each other irrespective of our degree of allegiance to the tradition.

I mix with a variety of committed people and have always tried to foster their working together and getting to know their real selves. The life-enhancing results for so-called opposites are a delight to witness. There are, I think, but relatively few who fail to recognize the immense contribution of people with limited knowledge of our tradition and who differ with us in other ways.

HC: I only hope that you're correct in that.

AP [with heightened intensity]: Let me give you an example that moved me greatly. A bus was taking me to a place I felt an obligation to visit here in Jerusalem. My attention was riveted by a father's outstanding behavior with a four-year-old boy, one of whose hands was missing. That boy's ceaseless, bubbling happiness with everything going on was a joy to behold. A still younger child was in a sling on the father's back. Since they were seated just in front of me, my inquiry about stopping-places beyond my destination made for a casual contact.

What I was witnessing caused me to continue on with them instead of proceeding to where I had thought I must be that day. What I discovered was that I had encountered only two of the four children who had been adopted by that exemplary, non-Orthodox father and his wife. As a young man, he had come to Israel from Yugoslavia where his mother had been a Partisan during the war. At the top of Masada [last Jewish outpost in war against Rome, 66–73] he met his wife-to-be, an Englishwoman. They are valued members of a communal settlement which, on principle, does not employ outside people. They do all the work themselves, including the running of a model guesthouse. Graciousness and helpfulness thrive there as well as in the facilities that are provided. That is how I found some new friends and Neve Ilan in the Jerusalem hills.

Thomas Hardy heard an uplifting song. The poet wrote about a bird that knew of some blessed hope of which he himself was unaware. In Jerusalem I have found myself surrounded by cause to be filled with a similar blessed hope.

The inner room at Anna Ticho Café had become crowded. We had been talking and eating for over an hour. Upon leaving, we walked a few blocks together to the Street of the Prophets. At the entrance to the garden at Helen Kagan's house, which we planned to visit, we were routed by two barking dogs. Undismayed, we entered the narrow street that leads to Mea Shearim.

AP: Now *this* is the bustling corner where taxis leave for Bnei Brak [religious suburb of Tel Aviv]. Each corner of Jerusalem has its own special flavor. It's good to learn their rich variety. And it's good to meet new friends like you.

HC: The immense pleasure has been mine.

I turned toward the center of the city, and Asenath Petrie—scientist, poet, lover of Jerusalem—headed for her home with its "view of a valley that leads straight to the sea." It was over a year later when I saw her next at her apartment in the Kiryat Moshe quarter of the city. Her leg was bound in a cast, and she had difficulty getting about. She was, however, in excellent spirits, and her poem "Winnowing Wind," which had been the Israeli entry in the 1986 Salute to the Arts international poetry contest organized by Triton College, was a first-place winner. It was featured in her new collection of poems, Whitening the Sunshine, *with which I was pleased to be presented.*

Rivka Miriam

Searching for Water

On a sunny but windy morning in early April 1986, I walked
slowly up Emek Refaim [*Valley of the Ghosts*], *the main thor-*
oughfare of Jerusalem's "German Colony," to the house of poet
Rivka Miriam. This is surely one of the pleasantest of Jerusalem's
older neighborhoods. Houses are substantial; there are many
trees, gardens, and spacious yards.

Rivka Miriam's house was set back from the street, ample
and solid. A squared-off structure which I had walked by many
times in the past, it looked older than it probably was. As she had
forewarned me over the phone, the name on the mailbox read
"Shereshevsky." A weathered inscription in German chiseled over
the front door lintel—PRAY FOR THE PEACE OF JERUSA-
LEM—I could half-decipher, half-guess, followed by its source
in the Book of Psalms. Inside, Rivka Miriam was expecting me.
So was Simcha, a very large, over-friendly dog. Attractive and
petite in her mid-30s, the poet tugged ponderous Simcha off me.
Her laughter and manner were rather girlish. She seated me in
the front parlor and left. In her absence, I looked around the dis-
tinctive room: the floor was boldly tiled and there was a profusion
of house plants, but it was the walls of the room that drew one's
attention. They were covered with large, Picasso-style drawings
of nudes, floating breasts, torsos, and doves wearing seraphic,
Buddha-like smiles. She returned bearing a tray of tea, choco-
lates, and pretzels.

Haim Chertok: That looks very good.
Rivka Miriam: So you live in Yeroham, the city on strike because there is no work for the people. Is it really so?
HC: Well, yes . . . and no. As I'm sure you know, nowadays
there is some work Jews either won't or can't seem to bring
themselves to do, or to work at together with Arabs, without
somehow losing face.
RM: What a shame! It was not always like that. At least until the
Six Day War, Jews and Arabs worked together.

HC: Yes, I know. A few months ago I spoke with Aryeh Liph-shitz, the writer. Do you know him? In his youth he worked as a stonemason here in Jerusalem.

RM: Of course I know him. I love him! He is eighty four and so full of life. I also know the pyschologist of Yeroham—Moshe Landsman.

HC: Moshe! He's my next-door neighbor and a very good friend.

RM: I thought so. My husband—he's the "Shereshevsky" writ-ten on the outside—is also a psychologist. They were class-mates together at Hebrew University.

HC: I never cease to be amazed how in Israel everyone seems to be no more than whistling distance from everyone else. Have you been writing for a long time?

RM: Oh yes. My father was Leib Ruchman, a Yiddish writer. He was a Holocaust survivor who came to Israel from Poland in 1950. I was born in 1952 here in Jerusalem, and I have lived here all of my life. Now my own three children are growing up here.

HC: If you were born a Ruchman and married a Shereshevsky, who is this "Miriam" person?

RM [smiles]: Oh, that's just a middle name that's now become my penname.

HC: What was it like for you to grow to adulthood in the house-hold of a writer?

RM: My parents' house was very special. Though my father was not a religious person, he had grown up, as it were, in the rabbi's courtyard. In his heart he was something of a *Hasid* all of his life. Our house was like the tent of Abraham the Patriarch, open at four corners to all kinds of people. They would come at all times and from all over the world with their kit bags to stay with us.

HC: How well did your mother manage in that situation?

RM: Oh, she didn't mind at all. Really. She was the inspiration, the real heart of the household. Without her, neither I nor my brother—he's a violinist—would have accomplished anything.

HC: Do you speak Yiddish?

RM: Yes. It was my first language. I still speak it with my mother.

HC: And how long have you been writing?

RM [smiling]: Oh, for a very long while. My first book of poetry was published when I was fourteen.

HC: Fourteen!

RM: Yes. A friend of my father's read my poems and liked them. He took them to a publisher in Tel Aviv. At first the publisher didn't believe that I had written them. He suspected that it was all a grand hoax, that they were really my father's work. He came here to see us. It was not so easy to persuade him that I was the poet.

HC: And since then?

RM: I have published five more books of poetry.

HC: I came across a few of your poems in English translation in a 1983 collection of contemporary Israeli poetry that Gabriel Levin edited for *The Literary Review,* an American quarterly. In fact I did a review of that special issue for *The Jerusalem Post* in which I noted that your poems were particularly impressive. I especially recall "The Stripes in Joseph's Coat." Have you published any collections of your poetry in English?

RM: No. You see, I don't push much. Some writers do, but once they are written, I really don't do anything more for my poems. Perhaps I should.

HC: How long have you lived here in this wonderful, old house?

RM: Five years now. It is wonderful, isn't it? When we bought it, it was like fulfilling a dream.

HC [gesturing toward the walls]: And you are the artist?

RM: Yes. I've been drawing since I was ten or eleven. I had my first exhibition at the old Tel Aviv Museum when I was seventeen.

HC: Do you think of yourself primarily as a poet-artist, an artist-poet—or something else entirely?

RM [smiles]: Sometimes I feel that I am nothing. [Pause] Maybe

I am more of a poet than an artist. Art is not the main thing with me, not the thing at the center of my life.

HC: It may not be the center, but you certainly have contrived to surround yourself with it. Judging from the walls, I would guess that you must be much taken with Picasso.

RM: That's true, but Picasso painted human figures that were broken, partial, not really wholes. I don't see things that way. I feel that everything is one. In fact, the more things are broken into pieces, into their smallest aspects, the more you realize or perceive that everything is really one thing.

HC: You sound more than a little like some nineteenth-century poets—American romantics like Bryant or Emerson. Many of Emerson's ideas about universality and oneness were borrowed from the East—that is, the Far East—and Hinduism.

RM: Well, maybe Judaism also comes from the East, or rather, I think it is the meeting place between the West and the East. My ideas, my feelings, are very Jewish. I feel very Jewish. The *Sh'ma* [Jewish affirmation of God's unity] is my source and expresses the essence of my ideas about oneness. I feel that the distance between things is very fragile. Our skins, our bodies are fragile fences, a border between us and others, between inside and outside. And there are times when I don't even feel this border at all; then everything merges into one. [Pause] There are other times when I really don't know.

HC: The texture of your poetry seems to me very different from that of many other talented Israeli poets of your generation. Tel Aviv poets like Menachem Ben, Maya Bejerano, Ronnie Someck seem to aim to sound exotic and offbeat, sometimes for their own sake. Moreover, their verse tends at times toward the confessional mode. Yours plainly does not, and in contrast to their poetry, yours radiates, positively exudes, Jewishness. I think almost every Rivka Miriam poem employs biblical themes in some fashion.

RM: That is true, but nevertheless I do feel close to many other of our young poets. It may sound a little bombastic, but you see, I feel close to every Jew: assimilated Jews, Orthodox Jews, aesthetic Jews—to all Jews. I feel at one with great rebellion, and I feel at one with great orthodoxy. Some of my closest friends are great anarchists; others are extremely Orthodox. I belong to them all. All labels are artificial, not real. Great rabbis have been doubters and great *apikorosim* [heretics] have been passionate believers. I belong inside no narrow frame at all.

HC [laughs]: Now you sound much like a female, Jewish Walt Whitman.

RM: Perhaps, but it is not to American poetry that I belong but to the Jewish people. To me being Jewish is not a frame but rather a stream that I flow on, that is conveying all of us. Sometimes I feel it so strongly it overcomes me. Each of us carries all of the Jewish generations inside of ourselves, in our very flesh: all the generations of the past and all generations to come. It is to me something awesome and powerful. I really feel that we are the very bridge between past and future.

Do not laugh! It is a great thing to be a bridge. When you think of it, all that Abraham and Moses did now depends upon us and no one else to carry on. We are the midwives, no, the very womb of the future. Perhaps that is why we are so long and so often in labor. Every nation and every person becomes much more powerful when they come in touch with their real nature and background, their reality prior to their being framed into the present time.

HC: There are a number of your poems which appear to issue from or express a position of religious doubt. I recall that in "The Stripes in Joseph's Coat" you have the God of the Hebrews sleeping, or at least dormant, while the idols under Rivka on the camel seem to be actively engaged in poking her.

RM: Yes, well, real life and real people tend to elude labels. After all, I should not make myself appear too mystical; I can at times also be very down-to-earth.

HC: I am sure. You say that you have three children?

RM: Yes.

HC: What sort of education have you and your husband chosen to provide for them?

RM: We follow the example of my father. Although he did not practice Orthodox Judaism, he sent my brother and me to religious schools, and I send my children to religious schools as well. Later, they will decide how to live for themselves. They will have an intelligent basis to make a decision. It won't matter all that much to me just what sort of Jews they choose to be. I am now, by the way, again in school myself.

HC: Oh?

RM: Yes, you have heard of the Shalom Hartmann Institute?

HC: Yes, of course.

RM: I am learning Talmud three days a week. I never have studied it before. I was sure, you know, that I didn't have a *Gemara kop* [good head for Talmudic study]. Now I find it strangely and wonderfully exciting, a great experience for me. The Talmud is very open, very undogmatic. It is almost surrealistic!

HC: Some of your poems also seem watered by surrealism. There are flighty images, such as the well rolling along in the desert which later itself rolls after the Israelites "like a carpet" in "Miriam's Well." That seems to me particularly striking. Surely you are also writing here about the poems in the well of Rivka Miriam and their succor for the Jewish people, are you not? [Smiles] You need not respond to that.

RM: There is, I suppose, a strain of surrealism in me. Just look at the walls of this room! In its own way, the Talmud can be just as wild. You can even find anarchists in it. In the Diaspora, Jews put their daily lives, which were often not so pleasant, into the deep freeze. Their real lives they saved for the Talmud. It is also a sensual book. There are endless ways to enter its many layers. Mainly, I most enjoy, I think, the Talmud's wildness. Yes, the *wildness* of the Talmud!

HC: Here is a wild, open, undogmatic question that you can answer from any approach you like. *How* do you write your poems?
RM [smiles]: Oh, I write whenever it comes. When it comes, it comes. I can't force it. Also, I never erase. I just write. Often I do not really understand how the images that I write work. It's as if the poems really have nothing to do with me. How they connect to my life, I do not know. I feel, in fact, more like an intermediary than a craftsperson. I never change what I write. If I don't like it, I throw it away. [Smiles] I throw away a great deal. Sometimes when later I read what I have written, I am really startled. I can even hate it.

You know, about seven years ago I was awarded a wonderful honor, one that Israeli writers crave. I received the Prime Minister's Award for my poetry. This granted me a stipend that allowed me to sit for a whole year without having to teach or do other outside work. Just to write. True, I had two little babies then, but still I had all this time.

At the end of the year, I encountered one of the judges who had given me the award. "*Nu* [Well], Rivka?," he asked. "How did it go? What have you produced?"

I was embarrassed to have to confess to him that in the whole year I had written nothing! But so it happened.
HC: Well, since I am merely the reader, let me say simply that I like what you have produced. Like much seventeenth-century English poetry, your poems are both religious and highly sensual. It's plain that they spring from a deep, pressing need.

Like the thirsty Israelites in need of quenching in "Miriam's Well," "The Girl Who Drowned in the Well" closes with "Lord, she was thirsty." And there is the power of the panting refrain in "Die in Me." Your poems insistently express craving for the real moisture of life as an urgent, vital matter.
RM: I think perhaps so. That is interesting to me, but I cannot tell you anything very interesting about the person who wrote my poems.

HC: Your poems are generally quite short, which, given the method of composition of the composer within you, is quite understandable. Have you ever undertaken a long poem?

RM: In fact, yes. About a year ago I wrote a long poem called "Jacob, Ladder, Rachel, Rivka." It depicts the meeting of Jacob and the ladder, but Jacob is sometimes Jacob, at other times Israel or Yankeleh [diminutive for Jacob], and at yet other times is one with Rachel. And there are three Rivkas: Rivka of the Bible, myself, and my grandmother Rivka—my father's mother who perished at Treblinka in the Holocaust. It seems very complex, but really it is simpler than it sounds to describe.

[A telephone call interrupted us. I paid scant attention until arrested by its final words: "*Ani nesheret b' Eretz Yisrael*—I'm staying in the Land of Israel."]

HC: Have you ever consciously expressed a social or political point of view in your poems or perhaps later discovered one imbedded between the lines?

RM: Not that I am aware. No poem of mine is political, per se.

HC: Do you work at an outside job?

RM: I take on occasional teaching assignments. To tell you the truth, I don't understand the first thing about money. I can't focus on it.

HC: What sort of teaching is it?

RM: I like to lead poetry workshops. In fact, I did a workshop last summer close to your home town at Yeroham. I worked with Chaim Meirsdorf, whom I think you must know.

HC: Well, that *is* a coincidence. I left him less than an hour ago. I stayed at his apartment at Har Nof [new Jerusalem neighborhood] last night.

RM: Really! I taught poetry-writing to the group of American youngsters he was trying to provide with a taste of the desert experience. It was very nice for me. The Board of Jewish Education of Chicago was the sponsor. My most recent workshop was for two months in Jerusalem. Among the students in the class was an old Yemenite poet; he wrote quite wonderfully.

HC: What did you think about the American youngsters or, for that matter, America's Jewish community? Have you been to the States?

RM: Another coincidence: I just returned last month from three weeks in America, my very first visit. I stayed in the East: New York, Philadelphia, Princeton, and Washington.

HC: Nu, Rivka, how did it go?

RM [smiles]: What can I say? It is very different. You can so easily get lost there. In some ways it can be great fun to lose yourself, don't you think? Here in Israel, I must face myself in the mirror every morning. I feel always a great weight. Since my childhood, in fact, I have felt, as I said before, that I personally am carrying the Jewish past and history on my shoulders and within me. It is not permissible to fall asleep even for a moment. You know, like a mother develops a third ear for hearing her baby's smallest murmur from the next room. That is what I feel I have when I am here in Israel. It is both delightful and painful. It belongs to me, and I belong to it: everything touches me.

As for your home country, I don't want to sound too anti-American—I am not—but American life seemed to me like jogging. Everywhere I saw people running all alone, closed off, with their Walkmans over their ears. It seemed so out of touch with the real. I sensed that people, that Jews in America, were very lonely. They shared no common pulse. Perhaps that is too superficial, but I could sense it. America was fun, but it doesn't really have much to attract me.

HC: Is that why you were saying *"Ani nesheret b'Eretz Yisrael"* a few minutes ago on the telephone?

RM: Yes. Just last week I was invited by the American Jewish Committee to return to America for another visit, this time to New York, Seattle, Dallas, and Washington, D.C. It is really an honor: though I did not think I had done so well in the interview, I was chosen as one of the four writers.

HC: What would be the aim of this visit?

RM: The purpose is to learn how the local American Jewish

communities are organized. It is very tempting because even though I would only be a special visitor and hardly really experience the Jewish life in these communities, still it would be for me like opening a window on a different reality. Imagine, for example, having the opportunity of opening a window, even a very small one, and seeing ancient Babylon, or Spain in the Jewish Golden Age, or seventeenth-century Poland! It would be a splendid gift. [Pause] But as you heard me tell my mother on the phone, *"Ani nesheret b'Eretz Yisrael."*

HC: Let me tempt you. You are missing a fine opportunity. Washington has splendid museums, and Seattle is a beautiful place of water: running through it, surrounding it, and falling most days from the heavens.

RM: So everyone tells me. But only after I was chosen did I realize how little I wanted to leave Israel. I don't need a vacation from here. I love it here. You know, I feel that we are living in the middle of a great historic time. Of course, because we are in the middle, we have no true perspective on it. Still, it is a privilege to be part of this era.

Not long ago I visited with a woman, an American, whom I had not seen in many years. While still in the United States, she had over heavy competition won a large grant in order to make educational video films. She is a very creative individual, a very special person. Then she married a fellow, a cook from Morocco, and went off to live with him on a *mitzpe* [hilltop settlement] in the Galilee. Years passed, very difficult years. Many people left their *garin*; there has been needless controversy. But she has stayed!

When I last saw her, she had a child about five and looked like maybe she was pregnant. Anyway, she has gotten larger. Her husband now works as a caterer in a nearby city. She was having a difficult time obtaining funds from the Education Ministry for equipment to make her educational video films which, had she stayed in America, she could have completed years ago!

One obstacle, one frustration after another. But she is there! She has stayed!

She did not say anything of great significance, only homely, ordinary things. But suddenly I realized—you must not laugh at this!—that I was in the presence of one of the great Jewish women of our era. A true heroine of Israel!

HC: Why should I laugh? I understand you perfectly.

RM: You could not possibly guess what we have in our backyard now? A mother and five baby *kipodim*. What is that in English?

HC: Hedgehogs.

RM: Yes, the cutest little hedgehogs. The mother hedgehog just appeared from nowhere in our backyard; we have made a nice home for her and her family. We called a friend of ours who is a naturalist and who writes nature books for children. He was so excited when he heard—apparently it is very unusual for *kipodim* to give birth in captivity—that he hurried right over with his wife, children, and camera. What really do I need another vacation for? Things like this are happening all the time to us here in Jerusalem.

HC: I have several American friends who have made *aliya* not so much to Israel as to your city of Jerusalem. And just yesterday I met a man, an American of course, who told me that he never, ever voluntarily leaves this special place. Perhaps your response to America is more that of a Jerusalemite than of an Israeli, per se.

You have lived here all of your life. You are so much of Jerusalem. Could it be that perhaps Tel Aviv is to you something like America?

RM [smiles]: Not at all. Our meetings of the Hebrew Writers Association get me to Tel Aviv fairly often. Of course I would not live there, but I like Tel Aviv very much. It is full of humor; Jerusalem doesn't have much of that—a sense of humor.

On second thought, however, there is a way in which you are correct. In Jerusalem, you know, one does not usually feel the present at all—only the past and the future. In America, and to a degree in Tel Aviv as well, you feel almost nothing but the present. Even much of the contemporary American art in museums seems like they just put frames around some everyday items. Things there are altogether too easy. They lack much value just because a special flavor must come from a sense of the past.

Now, as you know, here in Israel things are often quite the opposite of easy. Everything is a struggle. There is conflict and there is creation—nothing but crisis. It is like trying to give birth. We here are all like my *kipodim*, trying to give birth to ourselves. It is, as my friend said, very unusual.

HC: Do you enjoy your work as a functionary in the Hebrew Writers Association? It seems out of character for you. Also, organizations like that don't play much of a role in American letters. What is its real function here?

RM: Oh, I enjoy it well enough. It gives me an excuse to go away to Tel Aviv and to meet with other poets and writers. We discuss things of professional interest to us. Also we talk to people like copyright experts, publishers, and translators. Then we have to decide which of us should host visiting writers when they come. Many do come, you know.

HC: Could you imagine yourself not writing any more poems?

RM: Not really. It is so much a part of who and what I am. Moreover, since I believe that each generation is the gathering together of previous generations, all of us Jews are also that first Jewish poet. And it is my special luck and privilege to be alive, a poet and a mother, in this period of Jewish history because, for good and for bad, it is so very interesting. And I am a part of it.

Especially for us Jews, history has made its own selections. Perhaps some Jews need a kind of vacation from history. That is why some of them have left and will continue to leave us, even for good. [Smiles] America is our vacationland—is it not?—the place where our people can lose their sense of responsibility and

of time. At the same time, you and Moshe Landsman and Chaim
Meirsdorf and others have joined us here in our reality. Others
will in the future as well, I am sure.

I do not like to see Jews leave Israel, but I think we need a
larger perspective and not to be in anguish over it. History
makes its own selections for us. On the other hand, I often wonder how so many Jews abroad avoid feeling the uniqueness of
the period of history we are part of here in Israel. Never before
in modern history have Jews had so much to make and to do with
their bare hands as we do now. [Pause] But can you guess what
especially impressed me in America?

HC: The drug stores? The telephone service? Yes?

RM: No, really, you actually almost said it earlier. It was the rivers. The Hudson is so wonderfully broad. We have our Jordan,
of course, and I love it . . .

HC: . . . but it is [gesturing] like this little pinky compared to
the right arm of the Hudson. Right?

RM: Right, but I really mean something more. We Jews were
brought to this dry land, and that's why I think Jews always keep
running for water. That is the reason we have been the creators
of modern relativity physics and of psychoanalysis and of socialism and of almost every new and relevant recent movement.
People who live next to *real* bodies of water don't behave like
real Jews. Seattle would not really do for me.

You know, the Jewish man is circumcised at birth: all of his
life he will search for the missing part of himself, for water. It is
horrible to be missing a part of one's body, horrible always to be
thirsty, but it has made us creative. No, it is the Jordan which is
our proper stream.

HC: Have you any affinity for feminism as an idea or as a
movement?

RM: I feel that I am very much a woman. I think that there is a
genuine difference between men and women. I like this difference. Sometimes, however, I sense something masculine inside

of myself. Speaking generally, I think the feminine embodies
our human fruitfulness, the masculine our energy. I think that in
reality each of us, to varying degrees and at different times, is
both masculine and feminine. Perhaps in more creative people,
in people in the arts, the interior frontier between men and
women is much thinner.

HC: Thank you very much. Perhaps your brief encounter with
dry Yeroham last summer will draw you back again soon?

RM: It may be. Right now, though, I feel as though I am entering
a silent phase of withdrawal. I have had too much of public
situations lately. Possibly in the future.

But before you leave, you should have a look at our famous
hedgehogs. [She led me down the central hallway to the back of
the house and then outside to the backyard. In one half of a
wooden enclosure, about the size of a small melon, squatted a
stationary hedgehog. She bent down and, beneath an old garment, she disclosed five tiny hedgehogs.] Amazing, isn't it?

HC: Without a doubt. [Behind a partition in the same enclosure
were also two large turtles and 20 babies. We circled around to
the front of the yard.]

RM: Come again, and bring your family. And give my best
wishes to Moshe in Yeroham.

*Twenty months later Rivka Miriam and her family did return to
spend a Shabbat in Yeroham. In the interim she had published
another book of poems as well as a book of children's stories. Like
everyone else in Israel, we did not fail to talk about the Palestinian uprising in the territories.*

HC: Some aspects of the situation are bizarre. In Denmark, of
all places, P.L.O. supporters are intimidating supermarkets not
to stock Israeli grapefruits and avocados.

RM: It is terrible how suddenly isolated we seem to be. A good
friend of mine called from Norway. She said that she was the only
one she knew in her whole town who supported Israel. The only

one! It must, she thought, be connected to anti-Semitism. After all, the situation is not all that black and white.

HC: Still, didn't we squander twenty years during which we did not very actively pursue opportunities to come to some reasonable understanding with the Palestinians who actually live in the territories? At this stage, don't you think it would be best for us to disengage from them? For *our* good?

RM: I would like to believe that. If only I could believe that the Palestinians would be satisfied, I too would agree to let them have Judea and Samaria for their own homeland, their own state.

HC: You don't believe it?

RM: I would like to . . . but in my heart, I really do not. I think that they really want nothing less than everything.

Amos Oz

Off the Reservation

*Amos Oz was born in Jerusalem in 1939 and has been a member
of a kibbutz since 1958. Ever since the publication in 1968 of* My
Michael, *Oz has occupied a pre-eminent position among Israeli
novelists. Translations of his books have appeared in almost all
important Western languages (as well as the likes of Norwegian,
Catalan, Japanese, and Finnish). His newest fiction gets reviewed in journals such as* The New York Review of Books *and*
The New Republic *(where his 1985 novel* A Perfect Peace *was
touted as his finest work to date). Winner of numerous awards, his
most recent distinction came in 1986 when he was the co-recipient
(along with novelist Yitzhak Orpaz) of the prestigious Bialik Prize
for Literature.*

*Had it really taken nearly two years of sporadic letters and
calls to arrange this interview? Before departing from my home, I
checked. To be sure, my first note from Oz was dated in the summer of 1984: a first appointment was canceled because of his
speaking commitments for Shimon Peres in the national election
campaign. This was followed by a note announcing a sojourn
abroad, then one of purposeful isolation while he was finishing
a new novel. Finally there was a swatch of notes putting off a
scheduled meeting and signed by a secretary (not a good sign).
At last, three weeks after Oz had moved from Kibbutz Hulda-
Gordonia, in Central Israel, to the upgrade Negev town of Arad,
the time for the interview was fixed for a Tuesday afternoon on
what proved to be a rather warm day in June of 1986.*

*I arrived 20 minutes early at a comfortable, suburban-looking
street, from the crest of which could be viewed an auspicious vista
of the distant, brown hills. Oz ushered me cordially to a sofa in
an ample, windowless, book-dominated room whose entrance was
separate from the rest of the house. As best I could make out, this
was his office–study, a place intended for work and seclusion. His
residence and family were elsewhere in the town.*

*Looking perhaps five years younger than his 47 years, standing
a trifle under medium height, Oz is a handsome, even-featured,*

soft-spoken figure. Throughout our conversation, he was attentive, but his air was less warm than reserved. Perhaps he had
learned to practice caution with journalists. Was it despite or
rather because he had fashioned himself into a kibbutznik that his
manner seemed almost patrician? While he considered each reply,
some thoughtful lines creased the corners around his eyes. Ironically, his distinctive manner and address sometimes distracted
from the substance of his remarks: after each query he characteristically paused, considered, and then (if he felt the question war-
ranted serious response—not always the case) delivered himself
in measured, thoughtful, precisely modulated paragraphs.

Lending his words an oracular cast, between response and
follow-up question, there was usually total silence, a startling
absence of small talk which set him apart from the other writers I
had met or was to meet. Occasionally self-conscious but always
pleasant-mannered, Oz gives a memorable performance.

Haim Chertok: I'm sorry that I'm a bit early. My life is bound to
bus arrivals and departures.
Amos Oz: No matter. Come right in.
HC: Just finally getting to meet with you at all feels like a significant accomplishment.
AO: I apologize for seeming to play hard to get. That's not usually in my line, but the truth is that I *have* been putting off re-
quests for interviews for almost two years now. [Pause] I'm afraid
that all I can offer you is some warm tea from a thermos.
HC: Some cold water would be fine.
AO: Sorry, I don't even have access to a sink just at the moment.
HC: Well, then, let it be the tea from a thermos. Thank you. I've
enjoyed your fiction for many years, but have only had the opportunity to review you once: the *Until Daybreak* kibbutz story
collection that you edited and which contains your "The Way of
the Wind." It was in *Ariel.*
AO: Yes, I've seen it.
HC: How long now have you have been living here in Arad?

AO [without apology, lighting a cigarette, the first of several in the course of the hour]: Only three weeks. We are just settling down. It's to be a lengthy leave of absence from [Kibbutz] Hulda. We came here because my son's asthmatic condition was getting worse.

HC: I hope the clean air here helps him to improve. Does it feel strange to be living off the kibbutz for the first time since your youth?

AO: That's not entirely accurate. I have visited abroad fairly frequently—conferences, occasional sabbaticals at Oxford and in the States. As for Arad, it's really too early to say much. So far, my son seems to feel better here.

HC: How old is he?

AO: Eight. The doctors think that under proper conditions, the asthma could disappear when he reaches fifteen or sixteen.

HC [smiling]: If I had known about your problem sooner, I'm enough of an enthusiast that I might have tried to interest you in coming to my Yeroham instead of Arad. We don't pretend to be a model community, but we do have a particularly good climate for people with respiratory problems. It would have provided you and your family with a very different experience than will Arad.

AO: How long have you been living there?

HC: Almost nine years now—a veteran.

AO: And your family?

HC: We have four children: my daughter studies engineering at Ben-Gurion University and my son studies in a *yeshivat hesder* at Gush Etzion. They made *aliya* with us. Then there are our two *sabras* [native-born Israelis] who are now finishing the first and third grades. You have just one child?

AO: No, but as with you, our children came in two stages. Both of our grown-up daughters now live in Tel Aviv.

HC: I know that you were not born on a kibbutz. How old were you when you joined?

AO: I was fifteen when I made my personal October Revolution: I left home, came to Hulda, and chose the name Oz ["strength"]. I grew up, you see, in a rather right-wing, middle-class family in Jerusalem. I rebelled. My intention was to become an unintellectual peasant who works the land. [I gestured toward his book-lined walls, and he smiled.] Yes, I did not entirely succeed—an old story.

HC: My own as well. Before coming on *aliya,* I had taught English for fifteen years in American colleges. My wife and I became members of a *garin* that intended to set up an agricultural community. After a brave start with loading chickens, then some years of teaching from junior high to university levels, here I am—back with my pen and books.

Your primary kibbutz role was to teach, was it not?

AO: Yes, I have been a part-time teacher for twenty-five years.

HC: Discounting for the moment the communalism of the kibbutz: You would come closer than any other Israeli writer to making a living from your pen alone. Have you ever felt the temptation to follow the path of, say, a typically successful American novelist—that is, to write full-time?

AO: It's an intriguing possibility, but I confess to a failing: I *enjoy* teaching. I cannot even imagine myself as a full-time writer. I have a need for contact with people, to be in touch with them. Teaching seems to me a fair and proper exchange with other people. A writer in particular should not shut himself away from life. Further, if a teacher does his job properly, rather than just impose his wisdom upon young people, he has a fair chance to listen to them and to learn. [Pause] You no longer teach at all?

HC [head shaking negatively]: The wisdom of the Israeli classroom has done me in. Such is my confession. And this coming school year?

AO: It's likely that I'll be teaching Hebrew Literature at Ben-Gurion University, at least part-time.

HC: How do you deal with Amos Oz?

AO: I skip him.

HC: I'll alert my daughter anyway. May I ask you something personal which you quite justifiably might prefer to sidestep? [He nodded.] Continual friction—and worse—between parents and children, especially between fathers and sons, recurs repeatedly in your fiction. In *A Perfect Peace*, your most recent novel, the issue emerges in the matter of paternity itself. Are your own parents still alive?

AO: No.

HC: Did they, your father especially, ever come to understand or to sympathize with the values you espoused or the life you chose to lead?

AO: After some while, we did reach a kind of understanding. [Pause] There was a partial reconciliation.

HC: Let me shift to women as they appear in your fiction. Frequently they seem to be filled with a kind of violent energy or nervous eroticism. I'm thinking among others of Geula in "Nomad and Viper," the mother in "The Hill of Evil Counsel," and even of Hannah in *My Michael*. On the other hand, your male figures are typically more gentle and perhaps more passive, both more vulnerable and cooler. [Pause] This is perhaps a clumsy formulation on my part. Nevertheless, does it at all correspond to your own intent or self-perception?

AO: I suppose that it could be so, but even were it the case, any commentary about it would be the job of the critics rather than mine.

HC: Fair enough. Something less self-scrutinizing: no one could claim that you have been inhibited in using your experiences living on a kibbutz as material for your fiction. Do you view the kibbutz primarily as a refuge or retreat from larger Israeli society; or rather, do you see it more as a microcosm of our society and its problems?

AO: The kibbutz is a microcosm. I think that kibbutz life has some fascinating qualities. It is, of course, a kind of extended family. It enables one to get about as close up to a lot of people as one can imagine, desire, or perhaps bear. Within this setting, a relatively large number of people over a lengthy period of time establish, conduct, enter into and go out of a variety of sets of relationships far beyond what one may normally encounter anywhere else—more, at least, than is usual in the modern Western world.

   Having lived at Hulda over thirty years, I know a helluva lot about those people. I have of course paid the inevitable penalty for my knowledge: they know a lot about me.

HC: After more than twenty-five years, my second cousin is now in the process of leaving his kibbutz near Beit Shean. In some ways isn't the prospect of living away from the closed world of the kibbutz for the next four or five years, as it might have been for Yonatan in *A Perfect Peace,* just a bit of a relief?

AO [smiling]: No. I would not call it a relief.

HC: Would you agree with those who claim that the kibbutz is in a state of decline; that it has lost its ideological compass?

AO: Many of the old-timers have been saying for a long time that the kibbutz has been deteriorating. There are some among them who called the acquisition of our first "luxuries," private kettles for our rooms, "the beginning of the end." The kibbutz is now, however, a more relaxed society than it once was. There was once an almost messianic expectation that the kibbutz would change our actions and human nature. Another way is to be more moderate, evolutionary, and accepting. This is the way which I happen to prefer.

HC: I recently visited a very prosperous kibbutz here in the Negev, a producer of irrigation equipment. In these difficult economic times, is Hulda doing well?

AO: Not especially. Hulda is one of the smaller kibbutzim and is far from being very prosperous. This is not, by the way, a desirable condition. I don't believe that socialism necessarily means that everyone should be equally poor. Nor that economic well-being is necessarily opposed to idealism. I believe, in fact, that when we are more tolerant of each other's ideas, activities, personalities, and even whims, social conditions are more stable. The early founders, however, had a more monastic conception of kibbutz life.

HC: I'm not sure that I fully understand your use of "monastic," but let me pursue a related matter. In your novella *Late Love*, Shraga's letter to Hugo declares that the Jew is the inevitable recipient of the world's causeless hatred. It then attacks the Zionist myth of normalcy: "The Jewish people are totally unable to withdraw from the game once and for all. Did we really hope to take refuge here and build a new land and pretend to be a Bulgaria or New Zealand? . . . All the anger, all the misery, all the enthusiasm, all the hysteria, all the madness in the world . . . are all directed against us. . . ." How much distance do you put between yourself and Shraga, that is, between these sentiments and your own?

AO: Each and every character I create is close to me. Whenever I have an uncomplicated statement to make, I write an article. But when I am in disagreement with myself, when I am struggling, then I write a story. You would have no difficulty locating many contrary, even contradictory themes in my work.

As far as "normalcy" goes, Israel will never be a New Zealand simply because it is filled with Jews. Jews are not and never will be like New Zealanders. This country is still filled with dreamers and visionaries. We have living among us here millions of potential prime ministers, tens of thousands of potential prophets and messiahs. The key to our abnormalcy lies not outside but resides within us. This is often discomforting, but really, I would not want it much otherwise.

HC: You once said something to the effect that the Diaspora was in its way marvelous, but that after Auschwitz, we could no longer afford it. What is your feeling about Israelis who leave our country?

AO: Sadness. I have never felt like calling these people by insulting names, but I do think that those who have left Israel, and, for that matter, *all* those Jews who prefer to live outside of Israel, are simply missing the act. Israel, you see, is the only show in town, the only real Jewish drama now on the world's stage. Outside of Israel, no Jewish drama can come to grips with our central themes: Who are we? What are we all about?

Whether we put on a good show or a bad show is, of course, a wholly different question. It is true that some Jewish critics regard ours as a poor performance, as strictly third-rate theater. I take it that such is George Steiner's view, for example, and he is entitled to it. But still, he is functioning merely as the critic, and Jews outside rank prominently among our many critics. More than the actual substance of their reviews, *that* distinction seems to me of higher significance.

HC: It sounds as though your description of yourself some ten years ago as "a keen, sincere, determined Zionist rather than a cheerful, cheeky one" is still reasonably appropriate.

AO: In terms of collective Jewish creativity, the post-Holocaust Diaspora has been barren. So, when you think of it, must it be. Of course, individual Jewish creativity in many places still flourishes, sometimes, in fact, on an impressive scale, but individual creativity must always depend upon previous collective creativity. In this respect, individual Jewish creators in the Diaspora—to the extent that they remain Jewish, that is—are still spending the collective creativity of the non-existent Jewish centers of Eastern and Central Europe. They are living on an overdraft.

Since I don't see the remotest possibility of a significant collective Jewish creation emerging now in the Diaspora, it can only be a matter of time before individual Jewish creativity there also fades away. Jews may either come to Israel for inspiration, or else they may lose either their individual creativity or their Jewishness—or both.

HC: As you are doubtless aware, in the past year a small regiment of American Jewish commentators have written much-publicized books that have argued to the contrary. I'm thinking among others of Jacob Neusner, Charles Silverman, and most scathingly Bernard Avishai, who actually lived here for a period. Do you have any particular impressions about American Jewry or America at-large?

AO: I have visited and spoken there extensively. In some ways, America feels to me the least foreign of all foreign countries. Its tensions, even its agonies, evoke in me a certain feeling of kinship. But really, which America are we talking about? After all, America is too large and too abstract to generalize about.

HC: I'm not so sure, but let's return then to our own Lilliput. Several years ago you tersely summarized your reportorial tour *In the Land of Israel* with the comment, "The situation is not good." In the past four or five years, much has happened here. Has anything, in fact, really changed?

AO: I was very worried at the time about the level of emotionality in the public sphere and about the growing rift between the hawks and the doves, between the secular and the religious, and between the Arabs and the Jews. I remain worried, but I am glad to point out that these rifts should not be seen as synonymous with Israel. Our situation is much more like a puzzle than a football match. Perhaps the major achievement of the present government (of which I am not, by the way, very enthusiastic)—the major achievement of Shimon Peres personally—is in lowering the level of some of these inner hostilities in Israel. In particular, Ashkenazi–Sephardi temperatures have turned down.

HC: But hasn't the religious–secular struggle intensified?

AO: This tension, I believe, is the hardest problem of all. The bus stop burnings and synagogue desecrations are the tip of an iceberg. There is, however, something that our critics and we ourselves often overlook: other, much older nations, including highly civilized nations like blessed America, succeeded in establishing their underlying identity, in determining the ground rules of their national game, only after years of bloody civil wars. This has not happened here. Moreover, despite all our

nasty episodes of political violence, it is very unlikely to happen
here. Our Jewish violence in Israel is essential verbal. Our Jewish tendency is to give each other ulcers and heart attacks rather
than to shoot each other.

HC: And how do you account for us or, rather, for that tendency?
Is non-violence or non–physical violence the result of some governing spirit of Judaism or the Jewish religion?

AO: Judaism is not a religion; it is a civilization. Fortunately, we
have never had a Jewish pope. Our theology business being the
monopoly of neither God nor of any man, the name of our game
is interpretations and peripheral arguments. Further, with all
due respect, neither have I ever purchased the misconception of
identifying Judaism with *Yiddishkeit* [Jewishness]. Nor am I
ready to accept the idea that Judaism is restricted to *halacha*,
though with official Judaism at such a low ebb, we do live in a
low time. In better days, Jewish religious teachers were more
ready to argue and to put forward different interpretations of Judaism; readier, in fact, than were the official custodians of other
civilizations. In bad times, our teachers simply excommuni-
cated their opponents.

HC: My son's teachers at his yeshiva are rather open-minded
and much respected, but they generally understand their main
rabbinic function less as speaking out publically than as learning
and teaching. Unfortunately, some sort of rabbinic Gresham's
Law—rigidity driving out flexibility—seems to be the operative
principle in the present religious world. Those rabbis most
drawn to public life seem the very ones who are among the most
dogmatic. There have been better times, and not so long ago.

   A different matter: Meron Benvenisti's much-publicized *Data
Bank Report on the West Bank* conjectures that the weight of the
Jewish stake in the West Bank is such that either we now are
passing the point of no return for dealing equitably with Pales-
tinians or that we already have passed it. Not much land on the
West Bank remains negotiable, and the sands have run out.
How do you feel about this?

AO: I don't buy this analysis, which, by the way, seems to be becoming rather trendy among many who usually are thought of as adhering to the thoughtful Israeli Left. Death is irrevocable; very few other points of no return cannot be undone. We are talking essentially not about numbers of settlements and not about numbers of paved miles of highway. We are talking about a human state of mind and the human will. I do not believe that states of mind are ever irrevocable.

What Benvenisti's position most reflects, I think, is the depth of present frustration among Israeli doves, but I don't believe that it represents a sober reading of political realities. It is still possible, albeit under conditions very different from today's, to separate the heavily populated Arab areas from the Jewish ones and to carry out what I would describe as a fair and decent divorce between Israel and Palestine. It can still be done, and I believe that it should be done. [Pause] The trouble with a good many doves is that, deep down, they don't really want it to be done. They dream of an Israeli-Palestinian honeymoon and marriage, and disguise their romantic attitudes even from themselves behind the idea of "irrevocable realities."

HC: Are you hinting at a kind of psychological sabotage on the Left?

AO: I would not say "sabotage." However, there are those on the Left who are secretly enchanted by the Palestinian presence and are somehow attracted to their claims. I, for one, have never been impressed or attracted by Palestinian culture. I profoundly regret to say that the Palestinian National Movement is one of the ugliest and stupidest national movements in modern history. I still need to come to terms with it—and I will come to terms with it—but I do not need either to embrace or to endorse it.

HC: We started by discussing your writing, or rather, with you preferring not to talk about it all that much. Which I certainly understand. Still, may we circle round to it again? Who are the writers who have particularly influenced you, your style, or whom you have found of special importance?

AO: The Hebrew writers who I feel should be more widely appreciated—my own mentors, I suppose—are [Micha] Berdyczewski [1865–1921], Brenner, and, of course, Agnon.

HC: And on the world scene?

AO: That's too large an order.

HC: Well, whom of those you have read recently have you found impressive?

AO: The South Africans: Nadine Gordimer, J. M. Coetzee, and André Brink.

HC: You are not only much translated but your work, unlike that of many other Israeli writers, translates with particular grace. One reason, perhaps, is that your literary style seems to aim at being direct and uncluttered. In fact at the very end of *My Michael*, Hannah, dropping inflated rhetoric like "inner melody" and "alchemy," edits her own thoughts in a manner one might almost imagine an Amos Oz doing. Do you have any philosophy of literary style or approach to language?

AO: Frankly, I don't think about it much. Every novel begets its own appropriate style. Characters come to life within their own style. And yes, sometimes it happens that I have to straighten it out, to tame it.

HC: You have, I understand, recently completed a novel that you've been working on.

AO: Yes.

HC: Do you have a new project in mind?

AO: Not precisely. This is the time when I most feel like an old peasant woman who takes a vow not to get pregnant again.

HC: As Israel's best known and probably most successful novelist, you occupy what sometimes might prove a less than comfortable seat. While talking with other Israeli writers, I have occasionally picked up a discordant signal. [Pause] Perhaps you are familiar with the short story by Cynthia Ozick based on Isaac Bashevis Singer's parallel position among American Yiddish writers—"Envy . . ."?

AO: ". . . Or Yiddish in America," yes, I know it. Let me say this: current international interest in contemporary Israeli literature is remarkably high. One could almost speak of a breakthrough in the literary world for Hebrew literature in recent years. It is a good thing, and not undeserved: the Israeli literary scene may be among the most vivacious ones in the world. Now, I believe that the success of, say, one Icelandic writer does not exhaust the world's capacity to read other Icelanders. On the contrary, it stimulates the interest in readers everywhere to broaden their contact with whatever is going on in Iceland.

Envy, of course, is still envy, but objectively speaking, this is not the worst time for literature and for writers in Israel. With all due respect, our important work which still has not achieved its rightful world-wide reputation is that of the earlier generations, of Berdyczewski, Brenner, and the others.

HC [rising]: Thank you very much. It took a long time, but it was worth the wait. Before sending this off to the States, I'll mail you a copy so that you may make any necessary corrections.

AO [rising]: I would appreciate that. In the past I've read some comments of mine in print that I found most surprising and original. Now that I live in the Negev, perhaps I will find my way to Yeroham sometime in the future.

HC: That would be my special pleasure.

In fact, about a year later Oz did come to Yeroham where he presented a spirited lecture at the Cultural Center, which I of course attended. And since of late I too have resumed that "fair and proper exchange with other people" at Beersheba's Ben-Gurion University, our paths, albeit at some remove, have now and then intersected. Beyond his obvious intelligence and talent, Oz has done me several kindnesses, something not often associated with creative personalities of the first rank.

Natan Zach

Poetry Gloomier than the Man

It was a warm, sticky morning late in June of 1986 when I arrived at the busy corner of Dizengoff Street, my first return to Tel Aviv since my February meeting with Benjamin Tammuz. I had left his two novels in his electricity box, per plan, but I was now somewhat late for my appointment with poet—critic Natan Zach, one-time enfant terrible of Israeli literature, at the Café Frack. The Frack, Zach had informed me over the phone, was his café; if I did not recognize him from his jacket photos, I should ask the waitress to point him out.

Zach was born in Berlin in 1930 and arrived with his family in Palestine when still a young child. He emerged on the literary scene in the late Fifties with sharp, theoretical attacks on the reigning, flaccid conventions of Hebrew poetry. These were soon followed by two collections of his own relatively astringent verse. During the Sixties he had worked primarily in the theater. The following decade, however, was spent in England where he earned his doctorate. Returning to Israel in 1979, he began teaching at the University of Haifa and published North-Easterly, *a much-acclaimed volume of poems. In 1981, he was the recipient of the Bialik Prize, Israel's most prestigious literary award. The Static Element, a selection of earlier poetry, appeared in English the following year. Politically a man of the Left, for a long while he has been an outspoken critic of government policies.*

A waitress, noticing me confusedly glancing among the tables, approached. Was I perhaps looking for Natan Zach? He had called to say he would be detained. I should wait for him at his inside table.

I spent the next 20 minutes looking over my notes and the Dizengoff scene: girls in shorts, elderly men under brimmed caps, some tourists and stylish shoppers, buses, noise, crowds, and fumes. It was a downscale hybrid of Upper Broadway and Fifth Avenue. Nearby tables were occupied by older ladies eating pastries and drinking hot chocolate.

Finally, a man with a high forehead and pointy, academic

beard drew up. His left eye was badly discolored. It was Zach. He seated himself and launched in. It was plain at once that he was an expansive conversationalist, a raconteur. Breezy, anecdotal responses poured forth effortlessly. Much of the time he appeared to amuse himself.

Haim Chertok: I would have recognized you from the book jacket photo after all. Still, the waitress was very helpful.

Natan Zach: Forgive my lateness. I had to go to the infirmary to treat this sty over my eye. It's very painful.

HC: So I see. The fact is, I was late myself, but anyway, I was enjoying my chance to look over the passing show. I don't get up here from Yeroham very often.

NZ: I was last in Yeroham in 1957 while on reserve duty just after our crazy Suez adventure with the British and French. That's now over twenty-five years ago. There was not much there. When I left, I almost felt as though I had made an escape. They were engaging, as I recall, in some kind of protest over social conditions. You have been there for some time?

HC: Almost ten years. I think you'd find that things there have not changed too much. They—we—are still protesting. You're also an old hand at protesting, I believe. Oddly enough, Yeroham suits me. Even though I grew up in New York City, this city's climate and bustle simply do not. When I head out from Yeroham, I generally aim for Jerusalem.

NZ: I don't like Jerusalem. It's much too holy for me, makes me feel uneasy. I'm not really a snob, but especially since I don't drive, it's easier for me to contemplate traveling to London or Berlin than to Yeroham, Arad, or the other far corners of Israel.

HC: I commuted to Arad for over a year when I was teaching Israeli literature to foreign students at the WUJS Institute. In fact, I first became acquainted with your poetry when I taught you there. To me, however, Arad lacks interest and the scent of humanity. It's like a mechanical Swiss toy—a planner's fantasy.

NZ: Really? Now, I did go five months ago to Eilat for a lecture and reading. It was unimaginably hot, and the land so barren and red, it had qualities almost like a Fellini film. The atmosphere shimmers transparently clear; they say you can see for remarkable distances. Really extraordinary, but the heat was exhausting, and there were no trees. It may be my Berlin upbringing or the years in England, but a place with no trees seems to me uncivilized. I couldn't live there.

HC: Wasn't that desert film by Antonini *Red* something?

NZ: Yes, of course—*Red Clay.*

HC: You know, while waiting for you and looking out on Dizengoff, I had a small illumination. It struck me that this café could almost double for a different one that stood on the Grand Concourse of the Bronx which was, when I was growing up, a largely Jewish section of New York City. That café was a transposition of Vienna to the Bronx, a place filled with lady shoppers stopping for cocoa, gooey pastries, and gossip before riding home with their new purchases. It was called Sutter's; it's probably not there any longer. I haven't thought of it in decades.

The people passing here seem equally unvariegated. Not only are they all Jews, but they seem mostly of the same sort. Now in Jerusalem, I am always startled by the amazing variety of the passers-by.

NZ [laughing]: You have it exactly backward. Perhaps just now you see all these middle-class Ashkenazi faces from Russia and Germany, but on Friday and Saturday nights these streets belong to young, flashy Sephardim out looking for a good time. These Ashkenazi types totally desert the boulevards. When we come right down to it, perhaps Joseph Hayyim Brenner was most right about this place: he predicted that the country of Israel would become a national ghetto like any other Jewish ghetto. And certainly Bialik's cynicism has been vindicated: we not only have Jewish thieves and prostitutes; we have thousands of them. [Smiles] And they are probably among the best in the world.

HC: How long has this been *your* café?

NZ: The Frack is almost the last of a breed. There used to be half-a-dozen literary cafés in Tel Aviv where poets, theater people, and editors could comfortably gather. Most of them are now making more money as ice cream parlors—or even banks. Such is the fate of the Cassit, the café I used to frequent. Since they converted those nicer cafés, for about seven years the Frack has been the special place for a steady group of us, but even it hovers almost on the brink. [Pause] You came to Israel from New York?

HC: In fact, no. My wife is from Fresno, an Afula sort of city in Central California, and we lived in an even smaller town near there.

NZ: Fresno! I have been there! What a place for me! With its subways, New York presented no problem for a non-driver, but California cities were like prisons. I felt trapped.

HC: I should mention that I'm acquainted with Shula Yasny-Starkman who helped Peter Everwine translate your book *The Static Element.* She used to play guitar and sing Israeli songs to the children at Beth Israel Sunday School in Fresno. I assume your Fresno sojourn was connected with her.

NZ [smiles]: Of course, Shula and the guitar. She and Peter Everwine—they are now married—are currently visiting in Israel. Peter is enthralled with Israel. He is thinking seriously of taking an early retirement from the university in Fresno and settling here.

HC: Well, that would be one way of Shula's returning to Israel. Though I had not even heard of the word at the time, she was one of the first *yordim* I had ever met. I don't know her well, but tell her that you saw me.

NZ: Of course.

HC: Fresno is just a pleasant, provincial place, but for a time— with poets like Everwine, Robert Mezey, and Philip Levine— the university there had one of the most off-beat, stimulating

Departments of English in America. But let's turn to your work.
I came across an article you wrote two years ago called "Are We
All Dead?," in which you take to task Benjamin Tammuz, Amos
Oz, David Shabbtai, Yehoshua Kenaz, others—our most prominent novelists—for permitting their work to be dominated by
suicide and a parade of corpses. You urge them to be more wary
of death both in literature and in life. Do you really think that
you were fair?

NZ: Without question. The gloom and doom of recent fiction has
gotten much worse. It exceeds the darkness of our literature of
the Twenties.

HC: Yes, but don't you agree that writers are entitled to their
données? What is the good of exhorting writers to write about
something different? Would *you* pause to listen to such advice?

NZ: It's more complicated than mere literary advice. One thing I
did not know when I wrote that article was that Shabbtai was at
the time suffering from terminal heart disease. So *his* obsession
with death is understandable. Still, when I pointed out its manifestation in his writing, he himself was surprised. "I wasn't even
conscious of this," he told me. "You have made me aware."

HC: But all the Israeli writers you berate are not afflicted with
heart problems—or are they?

NZ: The trouble is that death and despair are part of our national mood. Our writers, however, should not project them onto
stories and novels where they often have no proper business.
Making them aware of this projection was my intent.

Now contributing to this condition is, I think, the discouragement and uneasiness with the reality of post-independence
Israel of the writers themselves. It is a reversal of the optimism
of the *Palmach* generation [the Forties] of writers who displayed
too high, wholly unrealistic expectations for our country. It reflects, as well, the cumulative effect of all our wars, the most
disastrous of which was the war in Lebanon. Particularly affected
were our army officers—a large proportion of whom are *kibbutz-*

nikim—and our intelligentsia, the preponderance of both of which are children of the Ashkenazim who for years were the leaders of Israel. There is hardly a family among them which has not suffered a direct loss to war or terrorism. This, after all, is Israel's natural elite; probably more in Israel than anywhere else do the intelligentsia, the writers, and the army officers spring from the same class. Believe me, among them the scent of death and discouragement is thick indeed.

HC: But it sounds to me as though you yourself have just isolated ample reason for this sour mood to permeate recent Israeli fiction.

NZ: Perhaps, but what we discover in these works is an unrealistic, frantic search for melodramatic effects. You see, the tradition of Hebrew literature is not really strongly rooted. Each generation of our writers has very largely started from scratch. Rejecting the pre-*Palmach* Hebrew models, the work of the *Palmach* generation writers is filled with causeless elation. But then, our expectations for statehood were unrealistic, almost messianic. We really lack the depth of the cultural tradition of Europe. A person with a historical sense does not expect so much . . .

HC: . . . or achieve so much either?

NZ: Perhaps, but he suffers less from the descent from high hopes to everyday bureaucracy and corruption. There is nothing romantic about our present situation and possibilities, a fact that people react to with a vengeance.

HC: But doesn't your own poem "The Taste of Hemlock" argue that "the hemlock's poison here is needed for remedy"?

NZ [roused]: Not at all! That poem is a reprimand against hemlock as dramatic remedy for our disappointments. I meant it ironically, again a victim, I suppose, of the translation. Yes, hemlock can also be a part of life, but it would be smarter for us Jews to stop expecting paradise. This is the cause of so much of our disappointment.

Nevertheless, the situation today is somewhat easier for us

poets than it is for our novelists, most of whom tend to search out foreign models. I think that the literary influence of the nineteenth-century Russian novelists, those masters of literary gesture and high drama, still exercises a strong, sometimes pernicious influence on our contemporary novelists. The Russians didn't write novels of growing up to manhood or English-style comedies of manners, and neither do we Israelis. [Laughs] It's really out of the question anyway, isn't it? In this country, we do not grow up, and we have no manners.

HC: You seem much attracted to English manners, but then you lived in England for longer than a decade. What really were you up to?

NZ: I left Israel after the Six Day War. You might say that I was recuperating abroad. I had had, after all, a cosmopolitan upbringing; I have little difficulty fitting in anywhere. Yes, I lived in England for eleven years. I went there to do my doctoral dissertation at the University of Essex and lived for my first three-and-a-half years in Colchester, the oldest city in England. So quiet and civilized; it was incredibly different, not an unpleasant change from Israel. The English really *do* sprinkle their conversation with pleasantries like "I say" and "don't you know?," and would you believe that I started to talk like that too. [Laughs] But I wasn't back in Israel for a week before all my acquired English manners vanished into the air.

More happens in a week in Israel than in a year in England. Who has time for "don't you knows?" In our little pressure-cooker state, all the polish and veneer falls away. Everyone here discovers everything about everyone else. An Israeli version of the Pollard affair would have been inconceivable: in our rattle-tattling country, everyone would have known. We Jews can keep no secrets from each other.

HC: In your opinion, would a person with what you call "a sense of history" perceive our Jewish history as somehow distinct or "special"?

NZ [smiles]: Of course. Jewish history is unlike all others, but this, perhaps paradoxically, is the very cause of that unhistoric, over-romantic vision of ourselves that afflicted the *Palmach* generation. The English have been rooted where they are for thousands of years. We Jews have moved from North Africa to Spain, from Spain to Germany, from Germany to Russia, and on, and on. We have not experienced a quiet, evolutionary process such as, say, the English or the Dutch. Except for our religion—which shows definite signs of final petrification—we do not really feel the lines of continuity in our history. Unlike the residents of European countries, Israelis have little confidence that they know what sort of place this country will really be in fifty years. We are still grounded in unreality.

Let me tell you an anecodote. About twenty-five years ago, when Eugene Ionesco came to Israel for a visit, he and I were walking here in Tel Aviv along Ben Yehuda Street. It was then a street with many Rumanian restaurants, and in short order, as you might expect, Ionesco was recognized. Now this was not in itself unusual, but after the restaurant owner enthusiastically invited him inside his establishment, can you guess what he had to say to Ionesco?

"Maestro, I have written a book that you must read."

Can you imagine! Ionesco enjoyed himself here tremendously. He once told me that people wondered how he thought up ideas for his plays, but that no place exceeded Israel as a living theater of the absurd.

HC: After ten years of living here, I am constrained to agree. However, you've chosen the English and the Dutch as examples of notably stable societies. Only a few weeks ago, when I went to Arad to talk with Amos Oz . . .

NZ: . . . Oz? What's he doing in Arad? Has he left his kibbutz? I didn't know that.

HC: Not exactly. His young son has a serious case of asthma, so Oz has taken an extended leave of absence from his kibbutz to live in a better climate. It will be a matter of some years. In any event, Oz had a somewhat different point to make when comparing Israel to other Western societies. He pointed out that we easily forget that countries like Great Britain, France, and the United States have achieved their relative stability only after civil war and much spilling of blood.

NZ: Oz has a more apocalyptic imagination than I; I don't dwell much on the question of civil war. I certainly do not expect that one will occur here. Do you know why? This place is just too small. A few years ago some Texas mayors came on a visit. When they heard about some of our problems, one of them boomed, "why, all this little ol' place needs is one good sheriff!"

No, the only real danger I can see is not civil conflict but from one of the madmen rulers, a Qaddafi or a Khomeini, who would be willing to risk our massive retaliation against his own people. Pakistan is already close to building an atomic bomb. Who can tell what a fanatic like Qaddafi or Khomeini would do with one? Calamity is a real possibility. For this eventuality, we who have served in the intelligence service know that all the talk about Israel's "strategic depth" is ridiculous. That is why we need to pursue a much more aggressive peace policy.

There is nothing like catastrophe to clarify reality so well: the Yom Kippur War, for example. I am sorry to say it, but we will probably need one or two more such jolts in the future. The truth is that it strengthened the peace camp. We had 200,000 people demonstrating in the streets. True, it split the country down the middle, but it had to be. After the Six Day War, people had been imagining that the Arabs would always be backward and ignorant, forever peasants or sitting in their cafés in their jellabas. Such is hardly the case; on the contrary, partly due to our sick economy, recently there has been a decided drop in educational levels here in Israel. But the Arabs, and especially Palestinians abroad, are rising educationally. In Berlin I met a Palestinian who was the head surgeon in a hospital.

HC: I know that you were born in Berlin, coming to Palestine when you were quite young. Earlier you mentioned that you had visited that city. How long ago was it, and how did it feel?

NZ: It was three years ago. That was my first time back in forty-nine years. Actually I came to Palestine not from Germany but from Italy. My mother was Italian; we left Berlin in 1934. I really don't have any recollections of the Berlin of my childhood, just a feeling for the atmosphere. After my parents arrived here, they never spoke a word of Hebrew—German, Italian, French, but no Hebrew. The cosmopolitan world of *Mittel-Europa* was the one that they brought with them to Israel.

As for going back to Berlin, it had simply happened that I had not returned. "Why?," I asked myself. I realize that I wanted to see it. Keeping my distance, you see, had never really been a boycott. I am simply a private person with no pretentions of being Spokesman for the Jewish victims and martyrs. So I went.

What I discovered is that Germans are more Jewish than I had realized, and vice versa. England is such a remote society, its Jews remain distinct.

HC: In your eleven years there, had you any connection with British Jewry?

NZ: None at all. German culture, however, has exercised an enormous influence on Jewish society. It was startling how Jewish so many Germans look. (I never experienced that sense in England.) It's part of the symbiosis of our two peoples. Aside from those twenty years—even less than twenty years—of madness, the influence of Germany and Austria on European Jewish society was stronger than that of any other. (The Russian and Polish Jews were largely isolated; they did not read Russian and Polish novels or such.) Did you know there were probably more great Jewish scholars, more Hebrew-language publishers in Berlin in the Twenties and Thirties than you could find in Jerusalem today? After all, our peoples did manage three hundred years of coexistence. It cannot, I think, simply be disowned. In sum, I think the natural affinity of the Jewish people to *Mittel-*European culture remains closer than, for obvious reasons, we are generally prepared to acknowledge. It will take more time.

HC: Perhaps. It does seem true that our distance from Arab or Eastern culture is not narrowing, even with people not opposed to rapprochement. When I spoke with A. B. Yehoshua, he mentioned that he had virtually no Haifa-Arab connections at all.

NZ: Yes, things used to be better. There was, I think, a feeling of greater closeness between Arabs and Jews back in the Forties. There was a Palestinian Arab writer I knew well, Rashid Hussein. He came from the landed Arab gentry, and he spoke perfect Hebrew. He and I collaborated on editing the first joint collection of Arabic and Hebrew folk songs—*Palm Trees and Dates.* We took our material from all over, even from the radio. Unfortunately, Rashid got too close to Hebrew and the Jews, and suffered all the bad experiences of an Arab in our Jewish Israel.

He wanted to rent a flat here in Tel Aviv. As soon as the landlord would hear his name—Rashid—it would be out of the question. He absolutely could not find a flat! Disheartened, he left Israel for New York where he became official Spokesman for the P.L.O. at the United Nations. All the same, whenever one of his old Israeli writer friends would come to New York, he would join him to talk about the old days and what was happening in Israel. Rashid drank too much. Finally, he committed suicide.

I think that things for Arab writers, however, might be somewhat easier today. Anton Shammas seems to be able to maneuver well. But then "Shammas" sounds very different from "Rashid Hussein," doesn't it? It could even be an Iraqi Jewish name. And his being a Christian instead of a Moslem must also help him to navigate. At an earlier time, Arabs were not allowed into the Writers Union.

HC: The *Hebrew* Writers Union.

NZ: Exactly. What royal battles were fought over that! Finally we created the *Israeli* Writers Union as an umbrella for all the non-Hebrew sections like the English writers, the Yiddish writers, the Rumanians, and the Arabs. But then the Yiddishists withdrew, returning to the main body. They were followed by

most of the others. [Laughs] I think in the end that the Arabic
writers and the English writers were left together.

HC: When you returned to Israel from England in 1979, were
you highly aware of changes that had occurred here?

NZ: Let me say that I think Israel's cultural horizons were more
expansive in the Forties and Fifties. People here felt more that
they belonged to a cosmopolitan world, a Mediterranean world
that included both us, even as an extension of the German cultural world, and the Arabs. All that is lost today. It has vanished. Many people here used to speak and read four or five
languages. In part as a late side-effect of the Holocaust, we are
psychologically and emotionally narrower and more isolation-
ist today.

There is one quite recent change: it used to be taboo to write
about the Holocaust. Later it surfaced as a theme in Israeli
poetry, but now it may be found in the younger generation of
novelists, such as David Grossman. However, the irony is that,
though the Germans now identify their destiny with that of Europe, we in Israel seem increasingly inward-looking and cut-off.

In England I was isolated. Something in me, however, enjoys
quiet. It was refreshing. I had no urge to publish what I wrote
there. On my return, I was ready for a major change. I got it!
Daily life in Israel can be so oppressive, so demanding. The moment I got here, I was tossed into the Israeli pressure cooker. It
was not long before we could scarcely remember England at all.

HC: You are married?

NZ: Divorced. Before going to England, I had been detached,
apolitical. I have now become more involved, but party politics
remain so obnoxious that I shy away from them as much as
possible.

HC: Almost two years ago, however, you were prominent among
a group of writers who publically opposed Labor's participation
in a National Unity government.

NZ: Yes, but once it came to pass, I relied on [Shimon] Peres to
make sure that the real differences between Labor and Likud

would remain intact, that nothing irretrievable would occur. Looking back, however, I think that perhaps I did not take sufficient account of how much the country truly needed a period of calm. That being the case, I would admit that those who favored the formation of the National Unity government were probably right.

Still, the underlying differences between our camps remain so real. In a matter of months, when [Yitzhak] Shamir takes over as prime minister, the Likud will probably heat things up again with the Arabs and even perhaps with the economy. If that happens, then the past two years would have been a mistake. Labor should not have extricated Likud from the mess they made of things merely to clear enough space for them to foul things up again. It would have been better for Likud to have failed so abysmally that, once and for all, they would have revealed their old, true selves: a permanent opposition organization of former terrorists.

If this latter scenario *does* come to pass, then Peres has done us all a serious disservice.

HC: The experience of talking with some writers, say Amos Oz or Carmi, is not unlike reading them. But you are something of a paradox: although your sense of today's Israel is almost dire and your poetry tends toward melancholy and preoccupation with the passage of time, your conversation overflows with good humor and high spirits.

NZ [laughing]: That's good. The poetry is, I hope, gloomier than the man. No, I suppose there is not much that is amusing in my poetry. It is my Jerusalem, my humorless place. There are, of course, changes, a development in my poetry that makes it difficult for me to talk about it as a bloc. An eternal problem resides here: the young man, the middle-aged man, and the old man— all three co-exist in me, in all of us. I suppose that part of me can be melancholy, but the larger part distrusts literature that indulges in gloom.

HC: You began your career as an outsider on the attack. Now you have won many literary awards, including the Bialik Prize. Do you feel as though you have become part of the literary or cultural establishment, even a bit co-opted by it?

NZ: Oh, I think the literary establishment still acts with a certain caution toward me. You know, I have attacked Labor, still the natural home of most Israeli writers, far more than I have Likud. Moreover, I think that I and my friends have had some effect. For example, Peres tried as hard as Shamir to prevent an investigation of the *Shin Bet* [General Security Service]. He was even comparing it [public furor when two captured terrorists were summarily executed] to the Dreyfus Affair! The noise we made has helped to ensure that an investigation will, after all, take place.

HC: Do you consider Zionism still a vital ideology?

NZ: Zionism certainly has an ambiguous history and origins. Its driving force was really messianic and unhistorical. And yet it happened in history: Israel is a fact! Still, George Steiner's recent critique of Zionism seems to me basically correct: Zionism has not developed an adequate contemporary ideology. Its course follows no logic.

HC: The Static Element, your selected poems in English translation, appeared in 1982. Are you at work on a new collection of your poems? What projects *are* you now engaged in?

NZ: I have not written any poetry for the past three years. It does not concern me. That's the way I have always worked, with big gaps and discontinuities. What I am now working on is a Hebrew translation of Allen Ginsberg's "Kaddish." I myself am not Beat Generation, of course, but I met Ginsberg in Israel back in 1959, and we became good friends. I later promised him to bring his "Kaddish" into Hebrew; the time has finally come.

I am also writing a book dealing with impressions of my visit to Germany. Yet another book will be essays on modern German literature, especially on the poems of Paul Celan. For a long time Celan kept a cool distance between himself and Israel. Then, at the time before the Six Day War, when it appeared as though Israel itself, standing alone, was teetering on the brink, Celan wrote a poem of identification with Israel. It was for him a kind of unambiguous credo which, strangely enough, was not well understood at the time.

HC: Perhaps most of our credos are more ambiguous than we think. Thank you very much for speaking so freely. I've enjoyed our talk very much.

Before I leave, I would be remiss without a confession. It was I who gave *The Static Element* such a lukewarm review in *The Jerusalem Post* when it first appeared. To my ear, the poems just did not work well in English. One funny thing: I didn't associate Shulamit-the-Translator with the Shula-the-Guitarist I once knew back in Fresno.

NZ: Ah, but you must read the poems in Hebrew. They are quite different.

HC: Doubtless, you are right.

NZ [turning to a nearby table]: Let me introduce you to some friends. [Four Frack regulars—an editor, a writer, a theater director, and an artist—pushed their table against ours and soon voices were ringing simultaneously. After a stretch of strained politeness, I departed for home.]

Zach's translation of "Kaddish" into Hebrew appeared early in 1988. Ginsberg made its publication the occasion for a return visit to Israel. He spoke widely, and was greeted with warmth.

Yitzhak Orpaz

Secular Pilgrim

In his early 60s, Yitzhak Orpaz is relatively little known outside of Israel. Only one novel—The Death of Lysanda *in 1970—along with a scattering of stories in academic journals (such as "Hunting for the Gazelle" in* The Triquarterly Review*) or in popular collections (like "The Wild Plant" in* Firstfruits: A Harvest of 25 Years of Israeli Writing*) have appeared in English. Since 1959, however, he has published twelve well-received novels and story collections, and he enjoys a high reputation in Israel for originality and a highly individual style. Writing in a parochial language has its frustrations and takes a special toll. Orpaz typifies the situation of a number of serious, ranking Israeli writers for whom international recognition has been slow in coming. In 1986 he shared the Bialik Prize, Israel's highest literary distinction, with Amos Oz.*

Back in 1981, I had favorably reviewed Orpaz's novella Ants *in* The Jerusalem Post *when it appeared in* The Iowa Review, *and we had had some intermittent contact over the years. He was born in the Soviet Union in 1923, emigrated to Israel in 1938, and, after some years on a kibbutz, worked thereafter as a builder, diamond cutter, journalist, and university lecturer. His apartment lies off a large square in North Tel Aviv, but, at his suggestion, our interview took place at a café in Jerusalem. It was a sunny day in early October 1986.*

Orpaz's face is deeply-lined, craggy; he doesn't smile easily. We spoke largely in Hebrew. More than most respondents, he seemed bent on getting certain things said, in leading our conversation along definite lines of his own.

Haim Chertok: It's good to see you again.
Yitzhak Orpaz: Other people have two feet. Every Jew has twenty. The trouble is deciding which foot to begin on. Let's just start.
HC: Good. What brings you now to Jerusalem?
YO: I shall be attending a performance this evening of a drama-

tization of my 1984 novel *A Charming Traitor.* This production won the first place award at the Acco [Acre] Festival of experimental drama a few months ago. In reality, just the very last part of the novel is dramatized. It deals with the problems of a sensitive young Israeli. Like many others of his generation, he feels drained of energy by the achievements of Israel's founding fathers. Still, everything is expected of him.

HC: Precisely why is he a "traitor"?

YO: Just that he deserts the expectations of family and friends. Deserts, in a formal sense, *all,* but nevertheless, everything he touches seems essentially to flower. He is at base good, but he can't feel strongly. He has suffered some kind of psychic injury. It all ends for him with suicide. The novel refers often to the Book of Daniel and Revelations. It is apocalyptic, an approach that I have always found congenial.

HC: It sounds reminiscent, at least in outline, of *fin-de-siècle* European literature, heavily burdened with fatality and doomed heroes.

YO: In a way, I suppose, yes. I intend him as an emblem of contemporary Israeli youth. They are sensitive, have lively ideals, but are wholly at a loss. Not long ago, one young man called me on the phone and declared that the play was absolutely about himself. It aims to express the inner personality of our young generation. Or, at the least, it expresses *one* pole, one part of the present Israeli condition.

HC: It's the pole your work in general seems particularly responsive to, wouldn't you say?

YO: Not exclusively, but perhaps more so. I treat this more fully in my philosophical book *The Secular Pilgrim* that was published in 1982. In it I envisage a kind of redemptive religious humanism. Unfortunately, it's not yet been translated.

HC: Why "religious" humanism rather than "Jewish" humanism?

YO: The way I see it, humanism is not particularly or peculiarly Jewish. It is universal, much of the sort of thing expressed by

Camus and Sartre among the existentialists. However, it does have, I think, a special Judaistic pathos. In my book, I describe two kinds of Jews that are healthy and balanced rather than schizoid: the ambassadors and the pilgrims. They are dialectical types. We need both of them to manage in the world. The book clarifies this idea of our Jewish pathos.

HC: And why this time "Jewish" pathos rather than "religious" pathos?

YO: In the way in which we Jews are always expecting something grand to happen, some final realization. It is a very strong Jewish category. Still, I grant that it is essentially universal. As a humanist, it is not enough to believe in the sanctity of human life but also in a conception of human life in itself as sanctifying. Only deeds, sacrifice, modesty, righting of wrongs, striving, and suffering really matter. Vulgar humanism is a gimmee, gimmee, gimmee faith of permissiveness. What is needed today is a humanism with teeth, something positive. *Shalom Achshuv* [Peace Now Movement] is too negative. It's always protesting against something and is always itself falling apart. This is a problem of the first importance. Of course, we must also guard today against racism, but that in itself is not enough. *Shalom Achshuv* reminds me of the Cheshire Cat in *Alice in Wonderland*: mysterious, aristocratic, beautiful, but finally a kind of effete phantasm. What's needed is a humanism with substance.

HC: How does your pilgrim philosophy fit in with other Israeli versions of humanism?

YO: I'm not entirely sure. I have tried to spread this conception to secularists like Shulamit Aloni and members of the Association of Jewish Humanists, as well as, of course, to students in my courses at Tel Aviv University.

HC: Then is it fair to call your humanism, in effect, your religious faith?

YO: The secular pilgrim searches for road signs telling him how to live. He learns both to recognize and to accept himself. It's really a way of life. Yes, religion *is* a formative influence. Although I am, after all, a secularist, the book is about the religious quest of secular writers.

My ideas got their origin in a course I taught at Tel Aviv University that analyzed three short stories—Camus' "The Gravestone," Hemingway's "The Killers," and Agnon's "The Infinity"—each from a phenomenological perspective. Each story features protagonists who are non-believers. What I discovered is that this kind of story emerges from conflicts which are irreconcilable and which can lead to no proper ending. As fictions they are, in reality, searches for an ending. Their actual endings are either fragmentary or illusory. For the writers, this is both a literary strategy and an existential situation. For the secular artist, it is I think an almost inevitable literary situation.

HC: And these stories imply religious quests?

YO: Absolutely. In Hemingway's story, the two killers function just like the two angels who appear at Sodom and Gomorrah. The story is informed by a secularized theology.

HC: Sticking primarily to work of yours that has appeared in English, how would you say this vision informs your own fiction?

YO: My books I think express a gothic detachment from past and future. In *The Death of Lysanda* the hero is detached, self-sufficient, strong. Insofar as my protagonist in "Hunting for the Gazelle" does not belong, he is a Jew. For good or for ill, I'm less severe than Hemingway. I refrain from bumping him off. *Ants* ends with the protagonist declaring "At last we were happy." This, of course, is meant to be ironic. It stands not for achievement but rather for an aspiration for purity, for spirituality in a secular world. And, in a way, they are happy. In my latest novel—the one tonight's play is taken from—my hero does indeed choose to die. This time, I let it happen.

HC: One critic I chanced to read thought that your ants symbolized the Palestinians forever chipping away at the foundation of the Zionist structure.

YO: That is, of course, too narrow, perhaps even a stupid interpretation. It certainly never occurred to me. [Pause] But in a
way, I suppose that it could be. Why not?

HC: Not long ago, I came across a very fine, rather sinuous short
descriptive piece of yours about the River Boog, the one in
which you seem to start, recapitulate, and inch ahead into a
prose poem of repetitions and variations. Like a musical work. It
was in a back issue of *Ariel*. Do you consider yourself "an experimental writer"?

YO: Oh, I am glad that you read that. I think it *is* a lovely piece.
Actually it was meant as the Introduction to a novel, but it
wasn't used. As for experimentation, I do experiment. I always
try to write in a different way, so insofar as I succeed, my writing
is always different. Critics really don't much like that. They like
to fit writers into formulae. So, I give trouble to my critics. They
tend, you know, to be lazy.

Once I got angry at a critic who saw the influence of Hemingway in my work. But now I must admit that the critic was correct. I hadn't been aware of it.

HC: The women in your fiction often seem to be monstrous. I'm
thinking specifically of the ladies in "Hunting for a Gazelle"
and *Ants*.

YO: Yes, they are like the women in *Gilgamesh*: menacing,
strong, and earthy. And yet it is a paradox. Actually, I consider
myself a feminist. I believe in women's equality.

HC: You've spent some time on campuses in America. How do
you feel about Israel's or Zionism's failure to attract large numbers of young American Jews, of the last decades' lost opportunities to augment our country's barely sufficient critical mass
of Jews?

YO: Zionism is *not* a lost opportunity. It's a grand success! But it
is passé, saying both too much and too little. We live in the
morning after. The Israeli sun, however, is like the Israeli nature—sudden. If Israel lasts fifty years, good. The Jewish State

is really a manifestation of the divisions of the Jews. It was Anatole France who described nations like persons: they're born, live, and die. A natural process.

Still, the Jewish people have experienced the enjoyable, paradoxical, historic fact of going from sickness to health. But from another point of view, our sickness was also our strength. Although we now live in the afterglow of Zionism, I am optimistic. We are now normal again. We have succeeded in creating a base in agriculture. We have raised a strong, young generation whose symbol is power. At the same time, Zionism as a motive force has exhausted itself. For its aspirations have been achieved. What we now feel is the depression after the peak. Philosophically speaking, the Jews are still a sick people. We need new health, a path away from unbalance and disproportion. Our difference is our spirituality, our non-conformism. The paradox is that the world increasingly resembles us Jews. If I am still optimistic, it is because I think that from now on our objective should be to conserve some of our abnormality. For you see, we never did become—nor will we become—quite like all the other nations.

HC: What was your general reaction to living in America?

YO: I was last there in 1978 at the International Writers Center at the University of Iowa. What can I say about America? It's a paradoxical place. I found Iowa too dry, too sterile, too ordinary, too clean. Only once did I see a girl holding flowers. I have the impression that the narrowness of America is now being imported to Israel. I spent last month in Spain. That's a different matter—much more stimulating. I made no connection to the American Jewish community whatsoever when I was in Iowa.

HC: Do you perceive any larger pattern to your own work or in your development as a writer?

YO: My novellas, my earlier work in general, are more abstract; my novels talk more of the here and now. But here biography and history intersect. In Israel, the Jew is born a second time. I came to this country when I was fifteen. It was perfect for me. I had had a terribly painful youth . . . very difficult. The sun in Israel scorched my past. I wanted to scorch it. My personal biography fit in perfectly with Zionism. It was as if I too began anew when I came here.

But when I first saw the Jordan River, you know I was shocked. In my imagination, the Jordan was the greatest river in the world. But there are really two Jordans. The original is still sustained in my imagination.

HC: And in your writing as well?

YO: Since the Yom Kippur War, there has been a looking back, a reversal. We are trying again to see what it was that we buried, the Jewish past and the Jewish condition. I too, along with the others. Some critics disapproved of *A House for One*—my first book after that war—in that I was suddenly dealing with personal material which seemed to embarrass them: with my family.

In *Tomozhenna Street*, which appeared in 1979, I tried to evoke a sense of timelessness in some interconnected tales of the town of Lipkiev in the years prior to the coming of World War One. Lipkiev is really a combination of two towns in the Ukraine: Zinkiev, my birthplace, and Lipkin, the birthplace of the Ba'al Shem Tov [Israel Ben Eliezer, 1700–1760, founder of Hasidism]. Did you know that I am in the direct line of the Ba'al Shem Tov? But in this autobiographical tendency I am very similar to A. B. Yehoshua who also has moved from more abstract to more realistic and personal work.

HC: What do you perceive as the proper relation between Israel and the Diaspora?

YO: I believe that Israel is really a branch of the Jewish condition of Diaspora. The Messiah has not yet come.

HC: And the growing divisions between us?

YO: I am against the splitting of Israel from the Diaspora. I greet that possibility with horror. Moreover, within this country of ours there may well yet be a civil war between the nationalist–fascist–messianic elements and the humanists.

HC: You think this a real possibility?

YO: Indeed! To some of those committed to *halacha,* the law of the state means less than nothing. Why is it that intelligent religious Jews don't fight *Kach* [violent anti-Arab movement] or Kahaneism more than they do? And why don't they just skip over the Book of Joshua when they teach the Bible? There's plenty of other material. There will, I fear, be a conflagration.

Perhaps it is unavoidable. My best hope that it won't occur is based less on rational prediction than on the paradoxical character of the Jewish people. My great fear is that we Jews will insist on both the entire Land of Israel *and* a Jewish country. The result will be apartheid. That's a monster. The Six Day War never ended. We are still living out the nightmare that began in 1967.

HC: It's a complicated matter. My own son now attends a *hesder* yeshiva which is located in Gush Etzion on the West Bank.

YO: And mine lives in a West Bank settlement also. But he's not a fanatic. He would move for peace, I am sure.

HC: How fully de-Judaized an Israel would you like to see?

YO: Well, there are limits. Even in a secular state, I couldn't imagine Jews not undergoing circumcision. It's our tribal ritual, like castration of the clitoris for some African tribes. On the other hand, I believe that we may yet be the center of new creeds, new beliefs for everyone. It's paradoxical: we still observe tribal rituals that are almost unbelievable.

HC: Have you an explanation?

YO: I have no logical answer. It's circular. To live a Jewish life is the basic characteristic of the Jew. Yet to be Jewish is the basic paradigm for all men. Look at Kafka. Exile is a pre-eminent Jewish feeling. Look at Hebrew literature. There's not one reasonably normal novel. Indeed, there's no such category in Hebrew as a normal novel. We have no Tolstoy. Our literature is extrinsic. The best of it is built on a teleologic formula.

Before Roth or Bellow, dozens of Hebrew and Yiddish writers wrote in the same way, writers like [M. Z.] Feierberg [1874–

1899] and Berdyczewski: a revolutionary approach always tending toward the future. In Jewish fiction, psychological questions are inappropriate. The real point of departure is, what is paining you? Where are you going? What kind of self-realization do you expect? So everything changes. You don't puzzle over a glass of water. You wait for redemption. This is the awareness that informs *The Secular Pilgrim*. [Smiling] I seem always to come around to it, don't I? It's really now the center of my life.

HC: You are now a man in your 60s. You have produced a substantial body of work. Are you satisfied, in general, with your relation to your readers?

YO: I shall tell you the truth. Until three or four years ago, my biography was a biography of misunderstanding. My critics did not grasp the theological dimension to my writing or my philosophy of Jewish history. It was like an anatomy of frigidity. What I was trying to say was overlooked. I myself could not understand my critics.

But now I must say "thank you," for in self-defense I was driven to write my own philosophical work. Happily, I'm discovering that people are taking it up. What is frustrating is that, although Dalya Bilu, the foremost Hebrew-to-English translator we have, would be happy to do the work, it remains untranslated. I cannot myself bear the cost of a translation out of pocket. This is a general problem for the writer working in Hebrew.

HC: What about the Hebrew langauge itself as a literary medium?

YO: Hebrew is different from French, English, or even Yiddish. They are like rivers. Hebrew, however, doesn't flow. Hebrew is stone. It is laid down, syllable by syllable.

HC: That reminds me of something similar that Aryeh Liphshitz once told me. Are you friendly with other Israeli writers?

YO: To tell you the truth, the better writers are not, I think, very friendly people. Oh, I feel close to Buly [A. B. Yehoshua], and once I did to Oz, though he's lately come to feel that he's the very voice of history. A kind of prophet. He used to be a *mensch* [real person]; now he's become a public personality. Too much rhetoric clogs his writing. You'll see it if you get to see him . . .

HC: . . . Well, in fact I . . .

YO: . . . He'll invite you to Hulda, his kibbutz, and point out the places that appear in his work, as if *he* had memorialized them. Then, of course, there's Yoram Kaniuk, though he's really something of a barbarian.

HC: Yes, well, enjoy your play and the plaudits this evening.

YO: Thank you. I intend to.

Early in 1988 I heard from Orpaz. He was recently back from a lengthy visit to France where, he was pleased to inform me, three of his books were soon to come out in translation. And a new book dealing with the Church and Christianity, The Eternal Bride, *would shortly be appearing in Israel. I reciprocated with news of the publication of my book,* Stealing Home: Israel Bound and Rebound, *in New York and, of more immediate interest to him, of the publication of his interview in the forthcoming issue of* Ariel *[Fall 1988].*

Elazar (Larry) Freifeld

Edited by God

Before moving from the United States to Israel in 1982, Larry Frei-
feld, who since his aliya *writes under the single name "Elazar,"*
published six collections of poetry. Through a mutual friend I re-
ceived a copy of A Jew in the House of Harvard, *his most recent*
collection. In 1986–87 it had received the First Prize award of
the Hebrew Writers Association for an English-language work. I
wrote a short, favorable review which I passed along to The Jerusalem Post. *An unexpected thing occurred: for unexplained rea-*
sons, the Post's *Poetry Editor refused to run the review. Mutually*
miffed, in late November 1987 Freifeld and I arranged to meet.

He lived one block from a very busy thoroughfare on the top
floor of a building in the very center of Tel Aviv, close to Bialik's
former house, now a museum. He was out when I arrived. I
chatted with his wife, Lois, herself a poet, who works as a high
school English teacher in nearby Holon. She had spent the pre-
vious Shabbat at a settlement on the West Bank. No, she hadn't
been frightened by the bus ride through the territories. "I'm
a religious Zionist," she declared. "There really aren't all that
many of us."

Unsurprisingly, the Freifeld living room and hallway were
filled with bookshelves. I noticed a computer in the adjoining
room. As we sat, their 9-year-old son burst in, home from school.
When her husband appeared, we all had tea.

In his early 40s, Freifeld is a compact, wiry man. He wears a
short beard, but more conspicuous are his contoured Italianate
glasses and a mellifluous voice.

Haim Chertok: It was dumb of the *Post* not to print the review of
A Jew in the House of Harvard, but I guess you don't travel in the
right company. I found much that I liked in it.
Elazar: It was annoying, but I'm not totally surprised. I've been
writing for a long time now and over the years have published a
lot. I know I'm a serious poet, so in the end it won't really make
any difference. I'm not boasting, just know what I know.

I'm a difficult kind of poet for poetry editors to classify. I'm a poet of the vernacular, of low language. Dennis Silk at the *Post* is not the first to experience difficulty with my work. Politically, the Right thinks I'm explosive while the Left considers me a fascist. Actually, they're all aspects of my collective personae.

HC: I met your explosive son. Do you have other children?

LF: Our younger daughter just went back to the States. She's supposed to come back in a month to enter the army. I hope that she comes. Our older daughter lives in Vermont, in Burlington. She studies at U.V. She was seventeen when we made *aliya*, perhaps a bit old for adjusting to a place like Israel.

HC: I was thirty-eight! Would you briefly characterize your poetry?

LF: I try to stick close to objective reality without being dull or prosaic. I also write fiction, by the way, but I was largely molded on expressionistic and concrete poetry. Earlier, when I was younger, I tended more toward the metaphysical/romantic. My poems now are often experimental, non-academic. The influences are not hard to identify. Certainly Whitman and Ginsberg. Also Blake.

Basically, I think the point of a poem is to communicate. I think of my poems as direct dramatic statements. I'm a narrative poet and rarely write in the first person except as an affectation or shielded by a persona. You know Swift said everything is a noun; I tend to range widely with pronouns. I don't believe that poets should get entangled in the delights of their own preciousness or delicacy. Like Baudelaire, I believe that there's an inherent music in the language. This is not something that can be learned. Maybe it's impossible. I think that over the years, having acquired the more formal aspects of writing verse, my own poetry has gotten more musical.

HC: Let's back up. What about your upbringing and education?

LF: I grew up in the Forties on New York's Lower East Side. It was then still a teeming Jewish neighborhood. Very poor. Lots of people lived in squalor in a very confined space. There were roaches and bedbugs inside and druggies in the hallways. I got into trouble in school and quit when I was eleven. Then I got involved for a while with street-gangs. Remember Marlon Brando with the pigeons on the roof in *On the Waterfront?* For a time, that was me.

I kept one step ahead of the truant officer and worked for booksellers on Fourth Avenue. Eventually I started my own mail-order book business, but that was later. They caught up with me and put me back in school, but in junior high I just went completely wild. A bit later, between the ages of sixteen and nineteen, I was arrested two . . . no, maybe three times.

I never did graduate from junior high school, but in the course of all my acting-up, I was noticed by the Assistant Superintendant of Schools and for a time became something of his protégé. He put me straight into high school, but I quit when I was seventeen. A few years ago, when I was thirty-eight, I passed the G.E.D. exams and finally earned my high school diploma.

HC: In addition to the Ba'al Shem Tov, you've written about such Jewish notables as Meyer Lansky, Arnold Rothstein, and "Lepke" Buchwalter. Do you think this fascination with Jewish criminals springs from your own confrontations with the law?

LF: I hardly think that four poems out of fifty-one could be called a "fascination with Jewish criminals." I think they're funny poems, some of the best in the book. We Jews also have our criminals. What's the problem? Just like most people, I'm a kid at heart who loves stories about outlaws and their adventures. Don't we all?

You know that story about Isaac Babel's Benya Krik? The young boy asks one of the old men of the village why Benya lives like a king when the rest of the Jews sit in squalor. The answer he gets from the old man is that while the rest of the Jews complain of their lot, Benya takes what he wants. It's like the old Yiddish saying *Vere m'chapt, dere erupt* [The one who grabs it is the one who has it].

HC: So far you've hardly mentioned being Jewish or what it meant to be a Jewish, Lower East Side street-kid.

LF: There's really not much to say. Most of my world was Jewish. Some gangs were Jewish, some were mixed, some had no Jews. My gang had some Jews, some Irish. But a certain degree of *Yiddishkeit* was just my natural condition, an accepted fact. I grew up speaking Yiddish, I went to *heder* [Hebrew school], and I had my *bar mitzvah*. Beyond that, I really didn't give being Jewish much thought.

HC: When actually did you first think you might become a poet?

LF: When I was fourteen or fifteen. On my own I was reading and studying Shakespeare, Milton, Blake, some Marvell. My early poems were imitations of Blake. Even when I was in jail, I read and wrote poetry . . . a dangerous activity in that environment. As I said, I worked for the book dealers along Fourth Avenue. Actually, I got my real education in their shops. I wrote book catalogues and, naturally, read through the offerings. [Chuckles] Once I worked briefly for a credit agency. I lost a check for $30,000. Naturally, I was perfunctorily fired.

When I got older, I moved to St. Marks Place. At the time it wasn't an "in" place. It was just an inexpensive neighborhood, a refuge from the high rents of the West Village, where artists, actors, and writers could live. I associated with people like Claes Oldenburg, Michael Steiner, Jerome Rothenberg, and Joel Oppenheimer. My career as a playwright began in the East Village cafés. In all, I've written twelve plays; three have been produced. I married Lois, who was an actress. That was in 1965. We traveled together in a company playing *The Diary of Anne Frank*. [Smiling in the direction of his wife] We're still happy together.

HC: And how did you keep from starving?

LF: Well, I also worked for a small New York publishing firm called Something Else Press. It lasted about ten years. It was a successful house that published, among others, Oldenburg, Rothenberg, Gertrude Stein, and theoretical prose pieces by John Cage. Also, I had a patron by the name of William Copley who liked my poetry, and in 1969 he helped me to obtain a grant from the Cassandra Foundation. At different points in my life angels like Copley have always turned up: Dick Higgins who owned Something Else Press, Michael Zinman who financed me to open a book store when I first came to Israel. Unfortunately, it went bankrupt after two years.

But that's getting way ahead. In 1970 we decided to leave New York for the country, which for us was Vermont. All in all, we lived there for twelve or thirteen years.

HC: Yes. In 1969 my wife and I left New York with a parallel idea. Before moving to Israel, we spent seven years in rural California.

LF: It seems to me that oscillation between city and country really does reflect a natural growth process of the mind.

HC: How did you survive in Vermont?

LF: In addition to writing poetry, I was a stringer for smalltown newspapers. We were involved with back-to-nature and assorted counter-cultural activities: food co-ops, Rochedale Community pioneering, simple living. I learned plumbing and carpentry. The last few years I was a mail-order, antiquarian book dealer. Possibly in response to living in a predominantly gentile environment for the first time, I also got active in the synagogue in St. Johnsbury (the big town in the area)—in Jewish politics and affairs.

Then an odd thing happened to us, perhaps a divine signal of sorts. In 1975 we were completely wiped out by fire. Books, paintings, manuscripts, furniture and clothes . . . everything except for one play manuscript. We were struck by lightning. Even when you know that your old work should be thrown away, it's tough to do. In this instance, I felt as though I'd been edited by God. That one play led me to believe that I should concentrate on writing plays for a while.

HC: How does the God who edited you connect to the God to Whom Jews traditionally pray?

LF: We all pray to the same God, don't we? I mean, there is only one God. He couldn't just be for the Jews; otherwise the world would be Jewish. Obviously, that's not the way He wanted it to be. Just look at Jerusalem!

HC: Okay. Let's go back to Vermont and your development as a poet?

LF: I published my first volume in 1964 in conjunction with the *Wagner Literary Magazine* poets. Its editor was a man named William Mass. He wanted me to change my name to Paul Blood.

HC: Paul *Blood*!

LF: Yes, he felt that Freifeld wasn't poetic enough. I didn't oblige him. That first book, one in a series called *Jonah*, was reviewed by Richard Eberhardt who wrote that I was "the most interesting poet in the series." Also, he warned me against "the excesses in Blake's later work." He was entirely right. The line length and rhythm of Blake's later work *were* revolutionary. Oceanic.

HC: That must have been gratifying for an unknown poet to read.

LF: More than just gratifying. Recognition by other poets, critics, just plain intelligent readers is essential. After all, none of us, except for Ginsberg and Bukowski, or someone like Rod McKuen, can really make a living entirely from our work. To a certain extent, mutual recognition takes the place of cash. It's vital. Without it, I think I would have switched to writing prose exclusively.

HC: Would you talk more concretely about the aims of the poetry you write?

LF: My feeling is that poetry is a revolutionary way of thinking. In the early Sixties, I was still consciously experimenting for the poetic form most appropriate for me. I recall that we were all very taken with the play aspect of making poems. For a while I used to work the poems out first on a chessboard. It was a sort of word-chess that would then get played out across a printed page:

a visual experiment with language. *Word-Chess*, in fact, is the title of one of my books that will probably never get published. Finally I came to the realization that for me, *what* was said had priority over *how*.

I think that I respond most readily to the oral tradition. This is a different sort of poetry from that written by some of the more "respectable" poets here in Israel. As I said, my poetic tradition is the vernacular rather than the literary: that is, the construction of the vernacular rather than the imitation of the literary.

As for *The Jerusalem Post*, I did, after all, win the annual award of the Hebrew Writers Federation. It's unfair of them to reserve the only English-language newspaper in the country for cliquish people who write the sort of respectable poems that were in fashion twenty–thirty years ago in London and the States. I know that my poems are direct, sometimes brutal, maybe even vulgar. I don't have much patience for literary conventions.

The whole situation is ironic, if not ridiculous. Younger Hebrew-language, Israeli poets tell me that the English language poetry that *they* are most interested in is the sort that I write, not the more academic, musty variety being written by connoisseurs at the *Post*. It reminds me of what Byron once wrote for his Preface to *English Bards and Scotch Reviewers*: ". . . I am not to be terrified by abuse, or bullied by reviewers. . . ."

But time is on my side. I'm happy to say that, despite it all, the book is selling well, especially in Jerusalem.

HC: And how does an English-language poet keep alive here in Israel?

LF: I do quite a bit of English editing—I recently finished a book for Masada Press—and I teach English at Gymnasium Herzliya.

HC: You like teaching?

LF: I enjoy the kids, but I don't much like what I get paid.

Moreover, all the administrative side of it is a waste of time. Except for the tests, most of the meetings I just don't bother with. Fortunately for me, there's a permanent shortage of good English teachers here, so they just put up with me. Anyway, I did a fair amount of teaching in the States: at the New School for Social Research and the Whitney School for the Arts. I'm also a proofreader.

HC: What about your current work?

LF: I think of my newest book as a kind of continuing panorama of the Jewish soul in its journey through the holy land of the heart, the mind, and the spirit. It's called *The Poet's Guide to the Holy Land.* It tends to deal less with the outer than with the inner world of reality. Its themes are love, war, and loss—especially of children. Like my politics—neither Right nor Left—it's difficult to categorize.

I suppose I write as much about violence as I do about love and peace. But isn't that what the world is about? I try to write about the world as it is, not as I would like it to be . . . though there's some of that in my book as well. I'm also working on a science fiction novel now, but lately my poetry's been going very well. In a relatively short stretch, I've written one hundred and twenty poems . . .

HC: . . . One hundred and twenty!

LF: Yes, most of them "Chronicles" of the sort I sprinkled throughout *A Jew in the House of Harvard.* The form is congenial to me. Just now I'm recovering from that creative binge, suffering a bit from something like the post-partum blues.

HC: How do you overcome the problem of writing for a foreign audience? Or better, whom do you take to be your audience?

LF: It's not something to overcome. After all, when I write in English in Israel, it's not as though I were writing a completely unknown tongue. English is the required second language here. Nevertheless, a general sense of loss is unmistakable and the vacuum hard to fill. Even as a Jew in my own country, it makes me feel like something of an exile. But the important thing is that I don't feel in exile *because* I'm a Jew. It's my own problem with the Hebrew language which is responsible for this loss.

But as far as the general situation of poets is concerned, it's better here in Israel than in the States. And despite the language barrier, there's this paradox: even though, particularly during the early Seventies, I was hardly an unknown in the States, I get greater respect and recognition for my work here in Israel. Experience has taught me to take my audience from wherever it comes. And naturally enough, like most Israeli enterprises, I look forward in the coming months to increasing my exports overseas.

HC: Let me inquire more directly into your bill of lading. In your long poem "*Haskala* [Jewish Enlightenment]: The Jewish Revolution in America," you pick up a gun to kill Nazis. Is this an ironic reference? In "Chronicles VIII" you decried all kinds of killing. Just two different moods, or is there some reconciliation here?

LF: It's really quite simple. I express through my poems a full gamut of emotional and political feeling. The problem lies in what you expect of me as a poet over and above what you know to be true about life or reality within yourself. What I'm saying is, I believe in killing selectively rather than senselessly or en masse. True, being a Jew, I am naturally inclined toward killing Nazis, more specifically perhaps, Nazi or enemy leadership. Neither for love of God nor for love of country, however, do I believe in killing populations.

Most poets come from the Left. So readers are conditioned into thinking that all poets are flowery, peaceable, innocuous— that they represent all "the better values." But we live in a complicated world, and I as a poet must be true both to my own inner voice and to the collective voice of my people. What puts me off about the Left is the constant underdog, loser's mentality. It's the sickness of the Left. Also, the Left is always disassembling, taking things apart, breaking things down.

The Right, on the other hand, represents a requisite, self-evident order and stability. If it lacks the intellectual stamina of the Left, it certainly offers to people with families, like myself, a sense of security and well-being. Ultimately, however, Left or Right depends for me on the specific issue at hand.

HC: How did you make it to Israel?

LF: As I think you can figure out from what I've told you, I'm a hustler. I can make it anywhere. As for the mechanics of the process, in 1981 we checked in with the *shaliach* [Israeli emissary] in Boston about a trial trip. Nothing came of it, so in 1982 we just came. We'd never been here before. I think it was more Lois' doing than mine. She's always been something of a closet Zionist. You know that great line of Moses Hess [German socialist, 1812–1875]: "Show me a dissatisfied woman, and I'll show you a Zionist." It's true.

HC: What's the most surprising or unexpected aspect about the lives you're leading in Israel?

LF: In a word, the people! In general, there seems to be a very wide gap between the perception of a thing and the action which ensues. Like their driving—positively nuts! Understandably, Israelis are all up-tight. And one has to get used to living under a largely socialist democracy as compared to America's capitalist democracy. There are some real differences: less human waste and deterioration, less crime, fewer hungry people, minimal alcoholism and drugs.

I wish, though, that Israelis would have more fun. Maybe a little decadence can be good for the soul. It would definitely be good for the arts.

HC: What are your present feelings about America or American Jewish life?

LF: I love the U.S.A.! Why shouldn't I? I was born there, grew up in freedom there. The States were always good to me. Of course, there's no perfect place, except maybe in *yenne velt* [the next world], and there are things I don't like about America, but so what? That's me!

The U.S., baby, is the greatest fucking country in the world, and you better believe it! But I feel no conflict of allegiance living here in Israel. In fact, it's my belief that one source of America's power is its people who are spread all around the world. As for the Jews of America, I harbor no resentment. I love Jews. We are a crazy, delightful people. We have our idiots, statesmen, millionaires, criminals, middle-class, whatever. Of course, I *would* like to see more come on *aliya*.

HC: You're happy here.

LF: Yeah, I like it. I'll tell you about Israel: I think you and I and others like us really share something of the heroic. What I mean is that, unlike most other American Jews who in their hearts also truly recognize that Israel is the center of Jewish history, we chose to come. We acted. That's the essential characteristic of the hero: the ability to put his own life on the line and to act accordingly. And since coming, I sense that my own vitality as a poet has greatly increased.

HC: About that, I know exactly what you mean.

LF [lighting a cigarette]: Do you mind?

HC: Go ahead.

LF: I feel very comfortable in Israel. [Chuckles] Sometimes I even feel like a King of the Jews. In this country, we're all crazy together. I'm at home. I'm productive. And I've been recognized, shown respect by established Israeli writers. You know you've arrived when your artist friends call you a Zionist pig. If you're ever in Tel Aviv on a Friday afternoon, that's when a lot of us gather together at *Beit Hasofer* [Writers' House]. You should come.

HC: You make it sound very inviting.

Yehoshua Kenaz

A-Zionist

It was the last calendar day of 1987 when I arose early to travel to Tel Aviv to meet with Yehoshua Kenaz. His latest novel, Heart Murmur, *had been the major Israeli best seller of the waning year. He lived on an obscure, one-block-long street in North Tel Aviv that no passers-by seemed acquainted with. Finally a butcher from his shop on Dizengoff Street directed me to the right street. I arrived at the apartment building barely on time.*

At the entrance, the stairway was blocked by a pleasant-looking man with close-cropped hair, wearing dark-framed glasses, who looked like the best friend in a vintage Hollywood movie. He seemed to be in his early 40s. Interrupting his flow of talk to a neighbor woman about something pertaining to building mainte-nance, he threw me a questioning glance. It had to be Kenaz.

"Haim Chertok, yes? Just a few moments, please."

As we mounted the stairway together, we encountered a second woman, with whom Kenaz had some other things to talk over. Evidently, Distinguished Writer Kenaz was also Good Neighbor Yehoshua. Finally we entered the apartment and settled down to talk. The living room featured a wall of books, many of them French. A second wall was covered with drawings, prints, and pre-Raphaelite etchings. A computer, familiarly beige, sat in the corner. To all appearances, it was a bachelor's apartment.

Kenaz's manner is natural, warm, and solicitous. He speaks rapidly in perfectly fluent English. Only twice during our conver-sation did he search the air for the more precise word.

Haim Chertok: It's good finally to get here. Emden Street must be one of Tel Aviv's great secrets.

Yehoshua Kenaz: After your journey up here from Yeroham, you'd surely like something to eat?

HC: No thank you, nothing. Today happens to be the Tenth of *Tevet* [Hebrew month]. I almost always observe the fasts: part of my compulsive nature. What I'm much less good at is checking the calendar before I make appointments to travel to Tel Aviv on fast days.

YK: Is it really the Tenth of *Tevet?* I'd lost track. Where shall we begin?

HC: Well, you're currently the top-selling author here in Israel, but you are still relatively unknown in the States, where this interview will probably first appear in one of the Jewish monthlies. Why not a brief summary of what you have written?

YK: Yes, I realized when you called that this interview would be for foreign consumption. I never grant them for the Israeli press. I find the idea of reading my own words in the Israeli dailies deeply disturbing, and not only because I know that inevitably there would be distortions. It strikes me somehow as a kind of unwelcome infringement. But for an American audience, I see little harm.

HC: Perhaps even some good?

YK [smiling]: Yes, perhaps some good. Let me see. A summary won't take me long. I write slowly. My first book was called *After the Holidays.* It had a fine success in Israel—it sold about 25,000—and very recently was issued by Harcourt Brace Jovanovich in the States.

HC: I know. A few months ago I read a review of it in *The Jerusalem Post.* Have you seen that review?

YK: No, I don't normally read the *Post,* but I have heard about it.

HC: The reviewer—I know him; he usually doesn't like very much—really savaged it, but, as the saying goes, it's an ill wind that doesn't blow some good. (There must be a Hebrew equivalent for that.) Ever since Benjamin Tammuz responded that he considered you among the very best of the younger Israeli writers, I'd been meaning to contact you. But close to two years have passed!

YK: That was good of him. He is a wonderful man and writer.

HC: Anyway, it was that damning review that goaded me finally to contact you.

YK: Yes, I see. An ill wind. But I don't pay attention to what gets printed in the *Post.* Of course, it pleases me to appear in an American edition, but once something gets translated, I don't feel that it any longer belongs to the author . . . and I'm speaking not just as a writer but as a professional translator. The readership I care about reads me in Hebrew, and the opinions that concern me are based on my original text. Language, after all, is not merely a neutral vehicle. For me, at any rate, it bears much of the message as well. In fact, it *is* much of the message.

Furthermore, don't forget that I wrote *After the Holidays* over twenty-five years ago! It first appeared in 1962 and has precious little to do with my current writing. [Pause] Nevertheless, I am pleased that Harcourt Brace reports that in America *The Los Angeles Times, The New York Times*, and some other important journals liked it very much. When all is said and done, that *Post* reviewer is of no serious consequence. My second book, which appeared in 1973, is called *The Great Woman of the Dream.* It hasn't been translated. Then in 1980 came a group of four novellas that I called *A Musical Moment.* One of them has appeared under that title in an English-language paperback collection, *Eight Great Hebrew Short Novels*, which was edited by Alan Lelchuk and Gershon Shaked. And finally there's my *Heart Murmur*, which has sold 40,000 copies so far, a smashing success for Israel.

HC: I should say. Including children and non-Hebrew readers, that's still one copy for every one hundred Israelis.

YK: A literal translation of the Hebrew title, *Hitganvut Yehidim*, would be something like "Single" or "One-Man Infiltration." It refers to a military maneuver they teach in infantry training whereby single soldiers steal behind enemy lines by themselves to capture a hill or position. The novel—it's my most ambitious so far—is about a group of new army recruits in the Israel of 1955. Naturally it presents their individual feelings and situation, which in turn reflect the general political and moral condition of the country at that time.

HC: Did you choose 1955 in order, perhaps, the better to write
about 1986?

YK: Some of it may reflect the present, but no, that isn't my general method.

HC: Before we get to your ideas or writings in detail, it'd be well
to establish your background. You were born in Israel?

YK: Oh yes. Both of my grandfathers were immigrants after
World War I, and my parents both arrived in Israel as children.
One side of the family is from Germany—really Galicia; the
other comes from Russia. They all settled in Petach Tikva and
soon worked in their own orchards.

HC: So unlike many other Israeli writers, you don't have a kibbutz background?

YK: No. . . . no kibbutz background! No Labor Zionist ideology
to rebel against! Like most people, my grandparents and parents
were *Mapainiks*—supporters of the Labor Party—but it was not
a strong ideological issue. Obviously, my grandparents had sufficient personal reasons to leave Europe and to come to Palestine, but neither politics nor ideology has ever been critical in
our family. You could call us Existential Zionists or even what I
consider myself today, "a-Zionists."

HC: You are an *a*-Zionist!

YK: Exactly, I grew up here. Hebrew is my language. This is my
country. That's all! It's all perfectly natural. As for all the Zionist
storm and controversy, it's just not my concern.

HC: Earlier when you mentioned the Hebrew language, you said
that it was not merely your vehicle. That it was also much the
point of what you wrote. Did you have a particular aesthetic or
some stylistic program in mind?

YK: Oh no! It's just that in my use of Hebrew, I try to be as exact
as possible. I work hard at that, and it adequately summarizes
my writing aesthetic—to be quite exact.

HC: Yehuda Amichai, it might interest you, responded in somewhat similar fashion. What about your education?

YK: After finishing my army service in 1958, I pursued a program in modern Middle Eastern Studies at Hebrew University. Then, when I was twenty-three, I went to live in Paris, a sojourn which completely altered my intellectual direction. I attended the Sorbonne and satiated myself, gorged on French literature, philosophy, culture. Then I started to write some stories of my own. I had never, you see, intended to be a writer at all. In fact, I had never been and still am not what you might call much of a reader, either. But as I said, the culture shock of Paris led me onto entirely new paths.

HC: Could you describe that process in greater detail?

YK: Well, bear in mind that I was an impressionable young man, for the first time in my life far away from home. It was the power, the cultural power of Paris, still at that time the undisputed center of the Western intellectual world, which completely dazzled and enthralled me. The ambition was born in me to conquer this culture—to dazzle it, to acquire it. Simultaneously, I did feel, at least from time to time, a poignant longing for *this* country, for Israel. The result was, I felt impelled to write. I sent a short story to Israel. It was accepted at once. This story became the first chapter of my first novel, *After the Holidays.*

I have been very, very lucky; some might say, very, very spoiled. It has been my good fortune that, from the very start, I have never collected any rejection slips. Perhaps it is because I have never written very much. In any event, I spent two years in Paris; I was quite in love with the place and with French culture. I still am. If ever I thought to live outside of Israel, it was at that time in my life. To remain was tempting, and if I *had* stayed longer, I know that I would have stayed for good.

HC: But you returned.

YK: Yes, after two years I returned to Israel, completed a degree in Romance Languages in Jerusalem, and continued writing stories and novels. I was also by that time translating French novels into Hebrew, something I'm still engaged in doing. But my decision to try to fashion myself into a writer, which meant a vital need for Hebrew as a living tongue, is what made the crucial difference for me personally. As a writer, the Hebrew language and the Hebrew-reading audience are what must be central, really critical. Now, at my age—I was born in 1937—I feel, quite simply, at home in Israel. It is home. [A telephone call interrupted us, and Kenaz spoke briefly with "Amos." I had a strong hunch who it was.]

HC: Where do you place yourself on the Israeli political spectrum?

YK: I should think that I am rather like most other Israeli writers and intellectuals. About the Palestinians in general, I agree with the position of the leftists.

HC: And how would you formulate it?

YK: Being, unlike most of my fellow writers, an a-Zionist, for me the basis for Israeliness, Israelihood—what shall we call it?— should be nationality, plain and simple.

HC: And Jewishness, the Law of Return?

YK: Really, who needs these problems that have no solutions? And what nonsense is all the furor over a Law of Return for people who don't want to return! That debate is all so pointless and non-productive. If we repealed the Law of Return, would it prevent a single Jew who wanted to come to this country from coming? Let's have a country with all kinds of people who become citizens because they are born here or really want to live here—all kinds of citizens. A pluralistic country like France or the United States. That really is my dream, Israel on the model of France.

Actually, even though it is philosophically a Zionist Party, I usually vote for Shulamit Aloni's Citizens' Rights Party. For the present, it seems to be the best tactic to vote on the basis of the protection and extension of civil rights to all citizens.

HC: Your pluralist vision sounds attractive, but how do you deal with the likelihood of an eventual Arab majority in such a polity?

YK: The question is for me an anachronism. After all, that would pose a danger for a Zionist State, but since I'm not a Zionist . . . Realistically, of course, I do see the present problem. We cannot simply erase the history of the past forty years. Still, if only in 1948 things had been done differently, my preference would now be for living in an Israel where it wouldn't matter whether our citizens were Arabs, Jews, Christians, or Buddhists.

But if there *were* a single Palestinian State embracing Jews and Arabs, there would be just one simple concession that I would fiercely bargain for. Perhaps it sounds very selfish of me but that one is Hebrew. Hebrew should always be the predominant cultural and official language of the country.

HC: How do you feel about Jews in the Diaspora?

YK: Very simply, I do not believe that this country can or should provide a solution to anyone's or any country's "Jewish problem." In principle, the very idea seems to me to border on the grotesque, as if Jewish history were some neurotic melodrama. About many things I can agree with Buly, but I certainly don't share his fixation about this matter. The Jewish community in France today flourishes as never before. How does that diminish me? On the contrary, if it makes them happy to live as Jews *and* as Frenchmen, well and good. Why should they feel guilty or constrained to come to live in Israel?

HC: What is your general feeling about the future of Israel?

YK: I can't claim to be very optimistic. The people ruling us are trying to kill the ideas of largeness, magnanimity, or even compromise in Israel. We are a small country, and we cannot long afford to be ruled over by such small people. [We again were briefly interrupted by the telephone; it was the writer's father.]

HC: Several years ago Natan Zach complained about contemporary Israeli writers, yourself prominently included, who seemed obsessed with morbidity and death as literary themes.

YK: Of course, I know the essay you're referring to; it has been much discussed. Zach voiced a legitimate concern, I believe, when he perceived the presence of death hovering over our literature. What he took to be an infatuation could, he feared, perhaps reflect a decadence similar to that which afflicted German society after World War One, in the days of the Weimar Republic. So he pointed to it. But, in fact, I am highly skeptical that death plays a more prominent role in recent Israeli fiction than it does in French, Italian, American, or other national fictions. *If* there is anything unusual going on, Israel reflects, I believe, the international cultural ambience. I find nothing fearsome in that. On the contrary . . .

Moreover, traditionally it is not the Left that has a fascination for death. It is the Right—*Gush Emunim* with its roots in Zionist Revisionism—that likes to prate mystically about Blood and Soil and Death. Speaking for myself alone, I have written about death for the same reason that I write about anything: because it interests me. I intend to write of it in the future without any real concern that it might become an obsession or preoccupation.

One aspect of death as a sort of Israeli public spectacle does, however, disturb me: the necrophiliac cult of *Yad Vashem* [Museum of the Holocaust], where all visiting dignitaries pay their *de rigueur* respects or shed a few tears. Starting particularly from the time of Menachem Begin and the War in Lebanon, the Holocaust has, I think, been scandalously exploited as a political alibi for almost any excess. My own immediate family was not victimized in the Holocaust. As for others, I prefer that they express their personal grief without transforming it into a national display. Don't misunderstand me, I don't criticize individuals who have suffered or who have suffered losses. But I hate to see the Holocaust used politically to purify disgusting actions.

HC: Let me turn to your fiction. *After the Holidays* revolves about two sisters and their father who live rather claustrophobic lives in a provincial settlement. It could be called "a family novel," but only in the way that *Wuthering Heights* might also be called a family novel. It is suffused by feelings of isolation, impotence, and frustration. Did you intend these marginal characters to symbolize some existential condition, similar to what we find in some of the fictions of Yitzhak Orpaz and Yoram Kaniuk; or perhaps, in the manner of Amos Oz, to stand for our national mood?

YK: No.

HC [pause]: Is that all?

YK [laughing]: No, but you see, I just don't think about or create my work in such terms. To tell the truth, I don't know how to deal with symbols. If I write about so-called marginal people, it is simply because they interest me. Similar remarks could be made about my latest novel, *Heart Murmur*: it is about the army, but the characters who particularly interest me are the eccentrics, the offbeat and the marginal ones. So they are the ones I write about.

Now that it's come up, a minor annoyance about the American edition of that book which reveals just how carelessly publicists read. The book jacket [rapidly scanning some bookshelves] . . . no, I don't have any copies of it here . . . claims that the action takes place before World War One. Actually, it plainly takes place *between* the two wars.

HC: In the current issue of *Tikkun*, an influential American Jewish periodical, a critic named Yael Feldman—probably an Israeli or ex-Israeli, she teaches at Columbia . . .

YK: . . . Yes, I think I have met her.

HC: She claims that the autobiographical and nostalgic mode now prevalent among Israeli novelists is in reality a displacement of Israel's political tensions into the personal arena. Then, along with recent novels by A. B. Yehoshua and David Grossman, she cites *Heart Murmur* as embodying a need for greater patience and tolerance with ourselves and with a rejection of unambiguous or quick solutions to Israel's insoluble predicaments.

YK: Offhand, I can think of a dozen recent novels and plays—writers like Yoram Kaniuk and Yehoshua Sobel—that deal directly with Israel's political problems. I, like most writers, I am sure, reject this sort of classification system. Naturally, Israel being a small country, most of us writers know one another, but I belong to no group or coterie of writers. Each novel that I write poses its own unique problems and gets written without any thought as to what other writers are doing. Critics and professors get paid to make these spurious connections. [Smiles] So much of it is really just so much rubbish.

HC: Who are your literary models? Judging from your bookshelves, I would guess them to be French.

YK: Yes, you are correct. When I was young, I didn't read extensively in classical Hebrew literature. That came only after I had begun my own writing. For me the two greatest Hebrew writers are Agnon and Yizhar [Smilansky, b. 1916]. As for the French [pointing behind him], my masters are Proust and François Mauriac. There are drawings of both of them hanging there on the wall. That one of Proust is his death mask. One American writer in particular, Sherwood Anderson, has made a major impression. I rather hope that he *has* influenced me.

HC: Yes, he is sometimes quite good, but I think not much in vogue now.

YK: I tend to like unfashionable writers.

HC: I as well. By the way, I almost forgot to ask what you do for a living.

YK [laughing]: Obviously you are no Marxist. Otherwise, that should have come first. I work at *Ha'aretz* as a sub-editor . . . you know, rewriting the material. I work there at nights. Then I also do a fair amount of translating from the French.

HC: Have any of your own books appeared yet in French?

YK: No, but as I said before, I have no particular desire that they should. I don't do anything to promote translations of my works. I might mention that I've composed most of my fiction when I was living abroad. For *Heart Murmur*, for example, I lived and worked in England for two-and-a-half years, on and off, in calm and comfort as the guest of the Oxford Centre for Hebrew Studies. I will always be immensely grateful to them.

HC: Have you ever visited the United States?

YK: I spent a brief period in New York, if that's America?

HC: Well . . . no!

YK: Still, it left a big impression. Truthfully, I'm not very familiar with American culture. Twice, I stayed for extended periods in England. But inevitably, abroad for me is France, or, speaking more broadly, the Mediterranean countries—Italy, Greece, Spain. I'm at home in the wine-drinking cultures; a stranger among the beer-drinkers.

HC: But surely you hoisted a few pints of ale at Oxford?

YK: Let's call Oxford a special case. At bottom, I am a Mediterranean.

HC: Thank you very much. It's time for me to leave Tel Aviv-by-the-Sea and return to Yeroham-in-the-Sand.

YK: But can I drive you to the station?

HC: Well, thank you. That would be helpful.

YK [driving a much-weathered Fiat 127 through the sunny streets of Tel Aviv]: You know, I adore this city, this Tel Aviv, and I was neither born here, nor did I go to university here. But I love its vitality, its movement, and the people.

HC: For me Tel Aviv plays Los Angeles to Jerusalem's San Francisco. When we lived in Central California, we always theoretically preferred San Francisco, but we often surprised ourselves by having a better time in L.A.

YK: On bright winter days like this, this city is marvelous.

HC: But what about the hot, muggy summers?

YK: Yes, they *are* terrible. Every year I promise myself to get away to a summer retreat in a dry, mild climate.

HC: Like Amos Oz in Arad?

YK [surprised]: Yes! He now lives there year-round, of course. I was, you know, speaking to him on the telephone just before. He has a wonderful place in Arad. Did you know that before 1967

Jerusalem also used to be a wonderful place? Unlike the shape-less sprawl of today, it was more like a small, European univer-sity city.

HC: And it houses far more hostility today than it did in the Seventies.

YK: Which means that it's been getting progressively worse!

HC: You're treading close to one of the biggest taboos in Israeli life—Jerusalem the Indivisible. Would you prefer to see a re-divided city if it were possessed of more charm and less strife?

YK: Let me put it this way: let the Palestinians have their part of it for a capital. No, I don't think the city should be physically separated again, but the Arabs will never relent if *their* Al Kuds [Jerusalem] remains under Israeli jurisdiction. No more than would be Jews. So many crazy people! So of course we should give them East Jerusalem for a capital for their own state. Simply enough, they need their own place—their own place to defend.

HC: Like Fatahland in 1982 Lebanon?

YK [smiling]: Exactly. That alone, I feel, could substantially change objective conditions. You must be getting a bit hungry or thirsty, no? Would you like to drink something?

HC: Not especially. It's only a half-day fast, not a twenty-six hour ordeal like on *Tisha B'Av* [day of mourning for the fallen Temple].

YK: I didn't mention that one of my grandfathers was a rabbi. He gave it up when he became an agriculturalist. After he arrived in Israel, he allowed his family to make *Tisha B'Av* just a half-day fast. It was the generation of my parents who gave up being reli-gious entirely. They associated it with the Diaspora. Like Yid-dish. Here you are. Have a nice journey!

HC: Thank you very much.

YK: Don't mention it.

Haim Be'er

Best Boy in the Class

On a Sunday afternoon in mid-February 1988, I was waiting in the café of Beit Hasofer *in Tel Aviv for my 5 o'clock rendezvous with Haim Be'er. For a change, I was quite early. With a wedding to attend that evening, I had given myself too little time for an effective interview, but I hoped that somehow Be'er would be early as well. His new novel dealing with the triumphalist wave of religious messianism in post-'67 Israel,* The Time of the Trimming [Et Hazamir], *had during the preceding two weeks sold a remarkable 30,000 copies. And in January, a dramatization of his first novel* Feathers [Notzot] *had officially opened Haifa's Festival of Israeli Theater to celebrate Israel's 40th year of independence. I had arranged our meeting by phone. He would know that I wore a beard; I, that he wore a* kippa. *Surely we would spot each other.*

In the adjoining lecture hall a very large, almost exclusively elderly, crowd had gathered. Curious which writer so many had come to hear, I discovered that the occasion was hardly a literary one. It was a gathering of pensioners from Germany. A legal representative was to clarify new regulations.

Shortly after 4:30 a round-faced, medium tall, somewhat stooped figure wearing jeans and a boyish smile scanned the large room, then seated himself at a corner table. After a few moments, I joined Be'er. He was already spooning a bowl of savory-looking pea soup. Throughout our conversation, before replying he would tilt his head at a reflective angle and pause, as if to consider his response with care. He spoke in a calm, rather soothing voice.

Haim Chertok: Haim, right?
Haim Be'er [smiling and momentarily rising]: Yes, Haim. I knew you would have a beard, but not a *kippa*.
HC: Yes. I should have mentioned it instead of the beard. There's no shortage of them, but I think we're the only two wearing *kippot* in the whole place.
HB: I came early purposely because you mentioned that you had a wedding to get to, so we couldn't possibly have very much time together.

HC: Obviously, my advance planning was hardly brilliant. We'll carry on in Hebrew?

HB: Yes, please. I understand English, but I don't speak it particularly well. And I can sympathize very easily with anyone writing under the pressure of time. I've just come here from the office of *Davar* where I filed my weekly column. *That* over with for another week, I can finally breathe more easily. Late Sunday afternoon is my time to relax.

HC: What sort of column is it?

HB: It deals with a variety of matters, but since it's mainly about books and authors, I call it "Memoirs of a Bookworm." I've been doing it for five years now. [Rising a bit, he waved a greeting to someone who had entered the café. During the course of the following hour, this occurred three or four more times.]

HC: Are you primarily, then, a journalist?

HB: Not really. I work as well as an editor at *Am Oved* [a publishing house], also for about five years.

HC: Since I'm familiar with your first novel, *Notzot*, which came out in 1980 I think, I probably know a good deal about your background. It reads, after all, very much like the memoir of a man recalling the impressionable boy he once was. Like you, he comes from a religious neighborhood in Jerusalem, and, with the help of an old man you called Mordechai Leder, he breaks out of his narrow confines. And like your current novel, *Et Hazamir*, *Notzot* was also a runaway best seller.

HB: *Notzot is*, of course, largely autobiographical. I was born in 1945 in Jerusalem and grew up there. My mother's family goes back to the old *Yishuv* [pre-State Jewish settlements]. It's been in the country over one hundred fifty years and can be traced back to the Gaon of Vilna [Elijah Ben Soloman Zalman, 1720–1797]. They first lived in Safed and later moved to Jerusalem. They were not really Zionists in the modern sense of the word. In fact, if anything, my mother's family was ultra-Orthodox and rather anti-Zionist.

My father's family came much later, from the Volin region of Russia. He was a storekeeper, a religious man but not an extremist. In matters of temperament, I am much like him. Though always Torah and *mitzvot* observant, my father was in some ways a child of the *Haskala*.

I was the only son, and I was educated in the state religious schools. Just like the boy in *Notzot,* though my house bordered on Geula [an ultra-Orthodox neighborhood] I moved spiritually in a direction away from the *haredim* [ultra-Orthodox].

HC: Which languages were spoken at home?

HB: My mother spoke Hebrew; my father mostly Hebrew and Yiddish. I grew up speaking a mixture of the two.

HC: And the army?

HB: It presented no problem. I served as a journalist attached to the rabbinical corps.

HC: Then writing for you goes way back.

HB: Oh yes. It's been a goal from my youth. When I got out of the army, I kept on with it. In fact, I bypassed university. So many years of study would, I felt, have been a waste of time. I decided to gamble everything on pursuing a career in writing.

HC: Going to university a waste of time? Many other Israeli writers have managed to combine academic and creative careers: Dan Pagis, Yitzhak Ben-Mordechai . . .

HB: . . . Well, perhaps I was obsessive, but I knew that I didn't want to spend my energies in the pursuit of an academic career, teaching, or literary analysis. Funny you should mention Dan Pagis. I discussed this very decision to skip university with him. First he reminded me of the old story about the danger of putting all of one's eggs into a single basket. But then he altered the tale by concluding that sometimes carrying one basket was the best way, or even the only way, to reach one's goal.

HC: He advised you to go for it.

HB [smiles]: Yes, to go for it!

HC: Well, you certainly seem to be winning your bet with life.

Even though *Et Hazamir* has gotten a cooler reception from the
critics than did *Notzot,* it's selling phenomenally. How would
you account for your books' tremendous popularity?

HB: I'll get back to the critics after a bit. The first thing I want to
say is that writing for me is primarily a way of self-discovery,
a means toward self-clarification. I write about what interests or
bothers me, and the surge toward messianism after our victory in
the Six Day War has been a matter which has preoccupied me
for years. So I wrote *Et Hazamir* because of an internal itch,
a pressure that kept driving at me. I felt that I had to. It's that
simple.

As for why it's so popular, I think that it's a very good book.
You know, I don't write all that much: just two novels, a book of
poems, and a book of literary travel essays. What I have tried to
do in my novels is to explore matters about which many people
seem to be sensitive, even touchy. Like a dentist, in *Et Hazamir*
I have poked around some raw nerves, and even though I have
heard very little yet from the West Bank settlers or the *Gush
Emunim* ideologues, I have obviously pained some of our literary critics.

HC: I'll return to your new novel in a bit, but before it slips past,
I'm curious about that book of travel essays.

HB: The title is precisely descriptive. They are essays occa-
sioned by my literary journeys to places like [Joseph Hayyim]
Brenner's house in London and the Swiss sanitorium in the Alps
that inspired Mann's *Magic Mountain.*

HC: Whom would you identify as literary influences?

HB: Let me think. As a youth, certainly Babel. Then Dostoev-
sky, Thomas Mann, and Agnon. He is very good. Later there are
Bulgakov and Gabriel García Márques. Also the Australian,
Patrick White.

Lately, I've been reading a lot of Flaubert. What interests me
in *Madame Bovary* is how he has so successfully focused on a
woman. My interest does not spring from feminist concerns so

much as matters in my own background. There is a lot of curiosity about women today. They seem more self-sacrificing than men. I'm interested in how this quality affects them internally. It may take a long time before this new direction of mine germinates into a new novel. In general, I need to think about new ideas a long time.

HC: In *Notzot* you describe a young man's passage from a parochial, orthodox world to the larger horizons of general culture. This is a common enough theme in European and twentieth-century American fiction. However, in Israeli fiction, I believe, it is rather rare. Do you ever suffer any regret about the path you have taken, about losing the comforting certainties of the world you have left behind?

HB: Who doesn't occasionally have regrets? But I have made my choices, and, married with three children, living in Tel Aviv I am content.

HC: To the best of my knowledge, English-speaking readers are still unfamiliar with your charming first novel. And how did you come up with that perfect title?

HB: You are right. Hillel Halkin translated the book into English a few years ago, but still no American publisher has been located.

HC: That seems strange. Perhaps now, after the commercial success of *Et Hazamir . . .*

HB: Perhaps. Oddly, the title of my first book posed for a time a major problem. There seemed endless possibilities. Finally I made a lengthy list of them all, among which was *Feathers of the Peacock*. Well, one day after synagogue I showed the list to my son, then aged seven. *He* wanted to name the book, which by that time seemed about as good a way as any to resolve the matter. He chose just *Notzot*, and so I dropped the peacock—all in all, a good decision.

HC: I agree.

HB: But the anecdote is really only half of the story. The point of the title is that feathers are the part of the body that gives one flight, which enables one to make an escape. On the other hand, feathers are also the dead part, the part of the body that lacks feeling.

HC: With that odd couple who still drink to Emperor Franz Joseph on his birthday, Riklin the gravedigger, Dr. Pele the Communist, vegetarians, Esperanto enthusiasts, and a variety of religious and comic types, *Notzot* displays an array of characters which makes your Jerusalem seem as rich and diverse as Dickens' London. As you've indicated, for personal reasons you now reside in Tel Aviv. But has it occurred to you that in leaving behind the richness of Jerusalem, you may also have abandoned the richest vein of your literary imagination?

HB: Well, my own wings have brought me to Tel Aviv where I have my work. It is obviously a symbolic as well as a practical choice. Naturally, there are both losses and gains. A feather tossed in the air never returns. But as I said before, I have no true regrets.

   You see, there were aspects to life in Jerusalem which I felt were choking me. I am not sorry for leaving that world. In some ways, there is, I think, a greater integration of different sorts of Jews here in Tel Aviv. [Smiles] Who knows: maybe the pace, the secular orbit, perhaps even the drunkenness of Tel Aviv are good for me?

HC: Though you continue to wear a *kippa*.

HB: Though I continue to wear a *kippa*. I am, after all, a selective person. Moreover, I have discovered in Tel Aviv much of what there was in Jerusalem. Still, there is surely a special character to this city as well.

HC: But it has not yet appealed to your creative sources. You have not written about it.

HB: No, not yet.

HC: Despite its comic elements, *Notzot*, especially for a *Bildungsroman*, has a singularly pessimistic tone. Yes, there are the utopian, life-enhancing figures like Popper and Leder, but they are more than balanced by the regressive, death-tending characters. In the end, the demise of Leder's son in the Yom Kippur War would seem to give dominion to Death.

HB: You have a point. I suppose that there is something in me that prevents my becoming an optimist.

HC: Let's move to your current novel, *Et Hazamir*, which deals with our messianic, national religious movement. What kind of "trimming" do you have in mind?

HB [smiling]: I intended a mild deception with my title. The reader's initial expectation would naturally be pastoral because of the association of *zamir* with "singer" as in the verse in the Song of Songs, "the time of the nightingale." The title's primary reference, however, is to *zamir*'s second meaning—"trimming." This refers to the trimming of the vines. One traditional interpretation of *this* trimming connects it to the time of death and to the End of Days which is the time of redemption when the Messiah will come. And this is the chord the Six Day War struck among our proto-messianists here in Israel.

HC: And this is your main theme?

HB: Yes. Many of the leaders of *Gush Emunim* have been friends of mine since childhood. We played together, studied together, went to school together. I understand so well what drives them on and how they think. In the beginning, in fact for a short period just after the Six Day War, I myself was one of them. This is why this book has plagued me for so long.

Writing it has helped to dispatch a heavy burden, a kind of personal necessity. I had to get this dangerous germ of messianism out of my system and into the light to show and examine it both for others and for myself. Now that it is outside of me, I feel a sense not only of accomplishment but of profound relief. After all, for Jews messianism is not, as some would have it, merely a matter of extremism. It is not something outside of us, outside of the Jewish people. No, it expresses something very deep, very elemental about us. There is in its impulse something of the very genesis of ourselves as a people, a dream without which we would not have survived over the years.

HC: Other peoples have messiahs.

HB: Yes, but our idea has little or nothing to do with the Christian idea of Messiah. For us Jews, messianism is like a reflex. At the same time, while we must wait for the Messiah, we are deathly afraid of it. This idea has for thousands of years sustained the body of the Jewish people.

But if we get tired of waiting, if faith in the Messiah's coming breaks, what then? Suddenly the body gets sick, takes ill. That is what infected me and so many of my boyhood friends. Utopia escaped from its imaginative borders and became our very lives. Messiah became our feathers, and the dream of redemption broke out, escaped from the Jewish soul.

It is so understandable, but so dangerous. We have suddenly reverted to the mindset of the period of Shabbatai Zevi [17th-century Jewish pseudo-messiah], or of after the Second Temple—a time of apocalyptic ideas. Every people, of course, has dangerous tendencies, each, perhaps, its own special variety. Ours is fundamentalism. It is our monster from the basement. Sometimes the monster breaks out. We have only to think of the Nazis.

HC: There was an article in last Friday's *Post* by Professor Zvi Kurzweil which proposed that fundamentalism was alien to Judaism. As best I can recall, he argued that true fundamentalism begins with Christianity, with its need *to believe* literally in the Bible. A parallel situation prevails for Islam. In authentic Judaism, however, the central authority of the Oral Law and of *halacha* discourages Jews from believing in a strict adherence to the literal meaning of the text.

HB: He is right. *Halacha* is one of the brakes against the pull of messianism. In point of fact, however, in our days *halacha* is proving ineffective. Why? Perhaps it is too eclectic. Rav Shach [spiritual mentor of the non-Zionist Shas Party] is pitted against the forces of *Habbad* [outreach organ of Lubavitch *Hasidim*], *Gush Emunim*, and the chanters of "We Want Messiah Now." In this one particular, I am sympathetic with him and even with the *haredim* who are anti-Zionist. Of course, in other respects I find them stagnant, and I have put much distance between them and myself.

What we need is new ground between Kahaneism—that vulgarization of messianic Judaism—and Rav Shach. Someone with the authority of the Hazon Ish [Avraham Isaiah Karlitz, 1878–1953] who could combat the mystification of power which has occurred within the national-religious world. For a time before the war it seemed that the humanist Judaism of B'rit Shalom [organization seeking Jewish–Arab rapprochement]—of men like Franz Rosenzweig [theologian, 1886–1929], Martin Buber, Ernst Simon [educator, 1899–1988], Hugo Bergmann [philosopher, 1883–1975]—might have served. Their experience, their dream was very interesting.

But its demise was one bi-product of the Holocaust, and not only because most of the Jews of Europe were destroyed. Their annihilation signaled the destruction of the dream of humanistic Judaism as well. Most Jews could no longer believe in it. Today *Oz V'Shalom* [peace organization of observant Jews], their successors, are a very small, not especially influential group.

HC: What is your estimate of the true danger of Meir Kahane?

HB: I'm not at all afraid of Kahane, the man. But we must recognize that the simplistic, vulgar solutions to our dilemmas that he offers are, in these difficult days, increasingly appealing. Recently they held a mock election in my son's high school, a regular State Religious School. Something like eighty-five seats went to *Tehiya*, twelve went to *Kach*, six for *Mafdal* [National Religious Party], and only two for Labor: that makes one hundred and three seats for the nationalists and only two for those willing to compromise land for peace. Not of course in those proportions, but to a large extent the results do, I think, accurately reflect their parents' opinions. People *are* gravitating toward the extremes, both of Right and Left, because the extremes offer the comfort of solutions.

The Jewish people need the non-Zionist *haredim* on the one hand and the Zionist secularists on the other in order to counter the militancy of the national-religious camp. It is a strange configuration. The dialectic of the two may, with luck, pull us through these difficult times. We are living in the midst of a very dangerous time.

HC: No one would dispute that. [Be'er waved a perfunctory greeting to someone at another table.] Are you particularly friendly with other writers?

HB [laughing]: Oh no.

HC: Well, you seem to know most of the people sitting here.

HB: Of course I *know* them. After all, I work at *Am Oved*, a publishing house. I have to work with writers, and though I'm sure they may be fine persons in other respects, I mainly see them when their egos are sticking way out. Some of them even bother me on Shabbat when I keep a healthy distance from the publishing world. They relate to me as they would to an instrument. No, my general experience with authors is anything but positive.

HC: Then who are your closest friends here in Tel Aviv?

HB: Well, I'll tell you: I think I most enjoy the company of the Jews at my synagogue. They are workers, policemen, storekeepers—simple men, for the most part. Good Jews. The synagogue is a kind of extra-terrestrial place. We don't trespass too much on each other's lives. They don't ask me what I'm doing there. Still, the people who come there can be thoughtful and sympathetic, and they think about each other. They are my closest *hevra* [peer group].

HC: The father in *Notzot*, who may be said to symbolize Jewish Orthodoxy, cuts a relatively weak, ineffectual figure, and one critic has noted that, though the characters in *Et Hazamir* are predominantly religious, the religious spirit seems absent in the book.

HB: Yes. Well, I think that in reality religiosity today is deficient, or at least dormant in most forms of Judaism in today's Israel. In my experience, for very few worshipers is the basis of their Jewish religious practice an inner religious spirit or impulse. It doesn't express something deep. In fact, I have the feeling sometimes that the Jewish religious spirit here in Israel has succumbed to some kind of failure of nerve.

Such is the case, at least, among the Jews I am familiar with. Perhaps it is different with the Conservative or the Reform Jews.

HC: I wouldn't want to disappoint you, but I think not. In my town of Yeroham, however, we have a very sympathetic *minyan* [congregation or quorum] that includes both Ashkenazim and Sephardim.

HB: Yes, but I was talking about something deep. Sometimes I think that it is simply no longer there.

HC: What *do* you make of the critics' cool reception of your new novel?

HB: Naturally enough, I have given that some thought. Since it is my author's judgment that I have written a good book, what might be involved? First of all, everyone seemed to like *Notzot.* I think that that in itself is a contributing factor to the unenthusiastic reaction of many critics—though not of all of them, I should add—to *Et Hazamir.* (And many ordinary readers have gone out of their way to tell me how much they like the book.)

Secondly, *Notzot* was primarily a nostalgic look back at a Jerusalem boyhood, a generally upbeat book, I think. It upset hardly anyone. Now, the new novel is something else again. It does take a stand. Though I recognize that protagonists of both of my novels bear a resemblance to me, the hero of the new book is an altogether more powerful and controversial figure than was the protagonist in *Notzot.*

Finally, *Et Hazamir* depicts many who once were my close friends and who now feel they have found the path to Utopia.

Evil, in the book, does not wear horns. It comes from within the human heart. I think that critics such as Amos Elon and several others have in reality not dealt with the book I have written so much as with the impulse behind the book. Yet even Elon has called it a key to the future of Israel.

So, though both of my novels have sold very well, my present situation differs markedly from what it was after the publication of *Notzot*. Then I was like the best pupil in the class, the golden-haired one—a *good* boy. Everybody liked me. But do you know something? This time I feel better. *Et Hazamir* is a stronger book than *Notzot*. It has struck the exposed nerve that I aimed at, and the pain has provoked anger. All in all, I am not dissatisfied with the critical reaction.

HC: Do you sympathize with the aspirations of the Palestinians? Have you taken a public stance?

HB: I am not as politically active as some other well-known writers. It is, I think, just a matter of temperament. In general, however, I may be counted among the doves. I believe that, given reasonable leadership, most Israelis would be willing to compromise with the Palestinians, and I am hopeful that something concrete will emerge from the disturbances in the territories. On both sides, the problem is one of leadership. I have no particular message or plan to add to the present public debate.

HC: What is your next project?

HB: I am currently editing an anthology of poems about Jerusalem. As for fiction, my first two novels covered a lot of new ground. My next book, however, won't deal primarily with ideas, with the past, or with society. I want simply to write a novel about a family.

HC: That reminds me: if I'm not going to be late for the *huppa* [wedding canopy], the time has come for me to be off. Thank you very much.

HB: Shalom, Haim. It's been a pleasure.

Yitzhak Ben-Mordechai

Sabra or Jew?

Early in March of 1988, I met with short-story writer Yitzhak Ben-Mordechai, my colleague at Ben-Gurion University at Beersheba. Youthful-looking despite a severely receding hairline, Ben-Mordechai offers the world an easy manner and an open smile. He currently was serving as Vice-Chairman of the Department of Hebrew Language and Literature.

On Time and Space, *his maiden collection of stories, was the winner of the Neumann Prize from Jerusalem's* Beit Hasofer, *and for the title story of his second collection,* Hunting Iguanas: Stories *(1979), he had received the Reuben Wallenrod Prize. Since then a third volume has appeared, and one of his stories ("Klein") was selected for inclusion in* Facing the Holocaust: Selected Israeli Fiction *(Jewish Publication Society, 1985). His work appears frequently in virtually all Israeli literary journals.*

Ben-Mordechai wore jeans and an unbuttoned shirt. We moved from his office to a faculty coffee room. In the far corner of the room sat a group that included Amos Oz, in his second year on the BGU faculty. Just the day before, three Palestinian terrorists had commandeered a bus on the Beersheba–Dimona highway: they and three Israeli civilians had been killed.

Haim Chertok: You are a *sabra,* am I right?
Yitzhak Ben-Mordechai: Yes. I was born in Tel Aviv in 1946. Not North Tel Aviv but in the proletarian southern part of the city, a neighborhood that must be something like New York's Lower East Side. My father was a simple man who worked in a bakery. The only thing he read was the Yiddish newspaper. In fact, there were hardly any books at all in our house.
HC: And how then do you account for Yitzhak Ben-Mordechai, Professor of Hebrew Literature and highly praised writer?
YBM: That's a good question. Sometimes I think being a writer is mostly a matter of genes. I have wanted to be a writer for as long as I can remember. You know, I wrote a story called "Family Affairs" . . .

HC: . . . Yes, I know it.

YBM: Good. The main character, Uncle Benjy, is a New York writer—both in Yiddish and in Hebrew—who in his last years, after his wife dies, comes to visit his family in Tel Aviv. Well, the story is very largely true. Uncle Benjy was my vital link to literature. When he was here, he got us tickets to plays and concerts and introduced me to the world of culture.

HC: There's an odd thing about that story: almost everyone except the narrator—the fiancée, the doctor, the wife—can get a fix on Uncle Benjy, but for the narrator he remains a mystery even after he commits suicide.

YBM [smiles]: That's me, the innocent one. When Uncle Benjy arrived in the 1950s, I couldn't see him clearly as the man he then had become. To me, he was a great man from the great world who sometimes acted erratically; indeed, he was my great hope.

HC: And yet the story ends with his suicide.

YBM: Well, as I said, it's based closely on actuality.

HC: Without a book in the house, what did you read?

YBM: Oh I read lots of romantic adventure books and stories by writers from the *Haskala.* I read almost everything I could. Looking back I sometimes think that I read too much as a youth.

When I got older I started reading more broadly: Agnon, Yizhar. Doestoevsky was important. Later, as a student at Hebrew University—that's where I took my degree—it wasn't the professors who excited me so much as listening to visiting writers like playwright Nissim Aloni who spoke with us. I got to know some of them.

HC: And your own writing?

YBM: I was a very late starter. Though I was storing lots of impressions, I didn't actually begin to write until I was nearly thirty. In fact, I was not at the time fully aware that I was even writing a story. There was to be an intensive summer workshop in writing at Haifa University. In order to join, you had to submit a sample of your work, and so it was then that I wrote what turned out to be "Family Affairs."

HC: Many of your stories, like "Klein" (depicting a woman's sexual fantasy transforming reality), "Haze" (about a girl's mysterious upbringing), and "Hunting Iguanas," present dream or obsessive material in conflict with the rational or common-sense world. Each time, the seeming reality succumbs to the power of obsession. Vitality and sexual energy, residing in the Kleins and Benjys and entailing primal images of horses and reptiles, overwhelm the rational, more conventional characters. In "A House by the Sea," it even leads to murder.

YBM: Yes, that is how it goes in my stories. In my own life, I'm not quite so certain that this is how things work out. But there you are: when I write, it is the everyday world that gives way to a more powerful version of reality.

I am now, in fact, in the throes of writing my first novel. You'll be pleased to hear that it almost ideally verifies your hypothesis about my work. Nevertheless, I am consciously trying to walk between the raindrops of realism and fantasy, as the Hebrew expression goes. It concerns the *golem* [homunculus] of Jewish legend, the most famous version of which was created in the sixteenth century by the *Maharal* [Rabbi Judah Loew ben Bezalel, the Wonder Rabbi of Prague]. The protagonist is an ordinary Israeli guy, not very different from myself, whose grandmother has filled his head with stories about the family *golem*.

HC: The family *golem*? In the legend the *golem* is destroyed.

YBM: True, but his grandmother believed that it survived, and that it founded a *golem* dynasty through her family. She fills his head with her tales.

HC: The grandmother was also the informing agent in "Hunting Iguanas."

YBM: True. Anyway, her stories creep like a worm inside of him and fester. You see, he cannot understand how, when everyone around him was destroyed, his own father had survived in the camps during the Holocaust.

HC: He seems to resemble the rational characters in "Klein" and "Family Affairs," out of touch with their own feelings, their own inner reality.

YBM: Yes, that is true. The book is really about facing the truth about oneself, and, you can believe it, just now it is obsessing *me*. At night, or walking to campus, in breaks between classes, working out its details is what I catch myself thinking about.

HC: How would you trace or explain your own development as a writer?

YBM: One thing I can tell you at the start is that for me it seems to get not easier but harder. I think that is because I am now far more self-critical than once I was. At the start, writing for me was an impulsive business. Now I'm more selective and the process is altogether more cognitive.

On the other hand, I began with stories that were based closely on reality, on real people and events that had happened. Now my work increasingly moves toward the imaginary and dreamlike for its resolution. Nothing fantastic like science fiction, but still in the direction of the surrealistic. However, I remain primarily concerned with the nature of reality, especially of Jewish reality.

HC: In which aspects? You are not, I think, an observant Jew.

YBM: No, I am not a religious person. Still I incessantly ponder what it means to be a Jew, and Jewish identity is my central preoccupation. Am I a Jew or am I an Israeli? I puzzle over whether there is a special point to being here in Israel and what it might be. Might it not be better to live elsewhere?

I have a right to ask this question. Unlike my parents, unlike *olim*, I don't have to prove to anyone that I'm an Israeli. After all, I was born here. I have fought in Israel's wars. I am an officer in the reserves. *Olim* want to become Israelis—new people. They have to prove it to themselves and to others that they have changed, that they have become Israelis. Frankly, I'm not so sure that they really can succeed.

HC: It's curious. Yehoshua Kenaz's reaction to being a *sabra* is that his Israeli identity is so intrinsic or natural that he does not want or have to concern himself about it. It just *is*, an existential fact. He calls himself an a-Zionist.

YBM [smiles]: And I, on the other hand, cannot prevent myself from inspecting it from every possible angle.

HC: But your disjunctive *or* is disturbing. Why Jewish "or" Israeli instead of "and"?

YBM: I myself do not fully know. But it definitely poses itself to me as *or.* A *sabra*, you see, is not exactly a Jew. He's just a native of the country. And what about the traditionally distinctive Jewish qualities: modesty, cleverness, intellectuality? Somehow they all seem to be muted if not, at times, lost here altogether. Being just an Israeli is not enough. If we lose these virtues, what will be left?

I know that Israel will only have meaning if it's a "Jewish State," but I don't really know what that means. It's not the same as the religion. Israel is the creation of the forces of history, but I sense that for some time we have been going in the wrong direction. I am dissatisfied.

HC: There is much in what you're saying. Unfortunately, everyone is well-acquainted with the *sabra* stereotype: brash, ill-mannered know-it-alls. Maybe their ugly flowering is part of the price of statehood?

YBM: What troubles me is the possibility that the distinctive Jewish qualities which are attractive developed just *because* we lived in *galut*? In which case, maybe the better choice of a place to live really is in the Diaspora.

HC: Obviously, I would differ with you. I recall that the Israeli protagonist in your story "Poet of the Exile" almost remarks the same thing: "I wish I were Irish because then life would be so simple." Because I have some unsimple Irish friends in the States, I had to laugh at that one. Have you spent much time abroad, in the States in particular?

YBM: Oh yes. My first wife moved to the States, and I have children from that marriage whom I used to visit every summer in America. Oddly enough, I didn't have much contact with American Jews on my visits. I know them mainly from novels.

HC: If you were there during summers, the campuses, where you would most likely have encountered your Jewish academic peers, were dormant. Since as many as ninety per cent of American Jewish young people attend colleges where they encounter academic role models who are actively or passively assimilationist Jews, I've often thought that the campus is the prime disaster zone for Judaism in America. Which American Jewish novelists have you read?

YBM: All the better-known ones—Bellow, Malamud, Roth. There was an excellent Jewish writer in the Thirties named Daniel Fuchs. He wrote three novels I think are masterpieces. But you know, the book I most admire is by the other Roth— Henry. *Call It Sleep* has enormous impact. Not long ago it was translated into Hebrew.

HC: Perhaps it's because Roth describes life in the sort of neighborhood in which you grew up. A. B. Yehoshua made what seems to me an apt remark about what we could call "classic" American Jewish fiction. Nearly all of it is concerned with what it means to be an American more than a Jew. Much Israeli fiction, like your own, seems to me quite different, and that difference seems a striking clue to the nature of the two cultures.

YBM [tearing the rim off his emptied paper coffee-cup]: Perhaps so. The historical phenomenon of Jewish emigration and adaptation fascinates me. In fact, I did my doctorate on a Hebrew writer by the name of Wallenrod who was one of a group of Hebrew writers living in New York in the 1930s and '40s. There are scarcely any left, I think. They came from Russia and Poland, some after spending a year or so in Israel.

Who knows? Maybe the Diaspora Jewish type that so attracts me in reality scarcely even exists any more. In any event, we all think that we act logically, but actually we are governed largely by psychological and historical forces that we can barely begin to comprehend.

HC: Let me ask something else. How do the demands of teaching and of writing work themselves out in your life?

YBM: Well, I've been teaching at Ben-Gurion for ten years now, Hebrew Literature and Creative Writing. It was eight years ago that we moved from Jerusalem to the Negev. I like this university very much. Even though inevitably things are more established than they were a decade ago, this remains a relatively fresh university where I feel free to try out new ideas.

Moreover, unlike the general run of Hebrew Departments at other universities, ours at B.G.U. welcomes writers to the staff. Aharon Appelfeld has been here for many years, and now Amos Oz has joined us.

HC: But what I asked about were the conflicts between your teaching and your writing?

YBM: To be frank, I suppose I would prefer it if I were able only to write. Or at least, given the chance, I would like to try. But we writers also have to eat. As I said earlier, I am now at work on my novel. Frankly, one of my major aims with it is to reach out to a larger audience.

Writing does require an enormous amount of time and energy in order to think and work. Still, one of the great advantages of academic life is that it does enable one to carve out the necessary time.

HC: I once asked Amos Oz a similar question. His feeling was that teaching kept him in contact with people; also, if I recall correctly, that it was part of his social obligation, his personal social contract, as it were.

YBM: Yes. I can understand that. Nevertheless, it is a compromise. I have never tried to dwell just within my writing. As the New Testament says, "Render to Caesar what belongs to Caesar, to God what belongs to God." Something like that.

HC: In the States I used to teach Creative Writing. It can be fun. How do you find it here?

YBM: It's a very popular course, and there is a growing demand for it, but it *is* difficult to teach effectively. Usually I have a group of ten to fifteen students in the class. How we proceed depends in large measure on the group. We discuss the students' work both intellectually and emotionally. I start them writing about themselves, so it becomes a highly personal, a deep experience for the students. After a short while, a good group becomes something like a family.

HC: A perhaps embarrassing question: have you ever actually taught anyone to write?

YBM: Well, I offer suggestions and criticisms . . . but to be honest, a mediocre writer cannot be taught to write really well, and a good writer does not really need a university course.

HC: This winter has been a particularly trying one in Israel. I'm talking, of course, about more than the weather. Do you see any ray of hope?

YBM: Yes. Now at least we Israelis are talking about the Arabs. We are thinking more about what we are doing here. At least people today, I think, are doing more thinking.

HC: Last week a letter signed by Amos Oz, Amos Elon, Yehuda Amichai, and A. B. Yehoshua appeared in *The New York Times*. It urged American Jews to join the Israeli–Palestinian debate, to speak their minds publically.

YBM: I am most uncertain in my own mind what should be the connection between Israeli and Diaspora Jewry. The relationship is very complicated, and I really cannot say with precision what is right and what is wrong. Perhaps this is because I cannot really understand why they continue to sit out there instead of coming to Israel.

HC: Aryeh Liphshitz, the writer who died not long ago, was also preoccupied with the eighty per cent of the world's Jews who choose "to sit out there." He couldn't understand them. But earlier you seemed rather sympathetic with aspects of the Diaspora.

YBM: Yes, but what of it? Both are true, and life is full of contradictions. It is difficult for a person to become an immigrant. It takes a special person voluntarily to take it upon himself. The fact that we have a special word—*aliya*—for Jewish immigration to Israel is highly significant. It points to a recognition of the difficulty of the act of emigration. Finally, I am almost certain that I will never emigrate from here.

I knew Liphshitz. In fact he presented me with my first literary prize. He was of a different generation, and there is a big difference between Israeli generations. Yes, I've fought in its wars, but for me, Israel is mainly a fact rather than a mission. It would be different as well were I a Diaspora Jew; after all, I have never experienced anti-Semitism. That undoubtedly makes a significant difference. So I think as I do in large part because of the circumstances of my birth.

On the other hand, I also feel unique in this respect: many Israelis feel that it's much better to be an Israeli than a Jew. I feel differently. I don't share the myth of the *sabra*, the myth of the new Jew. I don't feel it. The myth was propelled by the War of Independence and reached its peak at the time of the Six Day War. But things changed after 1973, after the Yom Kippur War. This was a big event for us, in some ways even a spiritual event. We *sabras* began to realize we were not really supermen after all.

HC: And what about the "new Palestinians" and their perception of us! Just three months ago, at the time of the glider attack in the North, I wrote an article noting the significant change among Palestinians who suddenly were making a target of our invincible Israeli army. Now they take on our soldiers with stones every day in front of television cameras.

YBM: I do think a Palestinian state is needed, not just because of the Arab needs but because of our own. However, I have no clear answers about how to move toward one peacefully. Temperamentally, I am of the Left, but I am not a natural *Shalom Achshuv* type.

HC: Do any Arab students study Hebrew literature?

YBM: Some. I treat Arab students exactly the way I do Jewish ones. There's no difference in class. But today in the cafeteria I had a startling, rather troubling thought. I looked over at a group of Arab students talking mildly to each other. Here on campus we are polite to each other. Or perhaps "correct" would be a better adjective. What struck me was that the same young Arab who here is pleasant to my face might kill me without hesitation on a street in Ramallah.

There is something really bizarre in this situation. Here on campus, students study and work together, and most faculty make no distinction. There is no separation. Yet just by a shift in context, I cease being me and become instead a representative of the Jewish people. The pleasant young student becomes nothing but a representative Arab. We both are drained of our individuality. It is weird, confusing, and dangerous.

HC: Is Arabic literature taught at Ben-Gurion?

YBM: No, but it's only because of budgetary reasons. It's taught at other universities. Arabic language courses are offered.

HC: Is this a good moment or period in Hebrew literature?

YBM: There's never been a better time than the present. And I think I can understand why. The present social and political situation may be muddled, but that only exerts greater pressure on our writers to deal intelligently with the important questions. Each one may have his own obsession, but all the good ones are genuinely engaging our reality. You see, despite our uncertainties, our Israeli culture has greatly matured. It is more serious and more interesting. And if in the past, the best Hebrew was composed by Jews—like Agnon—who may have lived here but were really products of the Diaspora, only with the present generation has Hebrew fallen into the hands of us native-born Israelis.

There is also the paradox that, although Israeli culture has matured, there is still so little time to ponder what we are doing. This is a very eventful country. Yesterday's terrorist attack blots out last week's crisis, and next week it will probably sink into obscurity. Yet who we are, what we are doing, where we are going must be considered by someone. These are our most important questions. Perhaps that's why so many books are published in Israel and so many are purchased. Though the real mystery is where people find the time to read them.

The attendant made motions indicating that he wanted to close the coffee room. Amos Oz had left his reading glasses behind. As we made our departure, Ben-Mordechai took them for him.

HC: Do you number other writers among your close friends?

YBM: We are friendly. This is a small, close country. Everybody knows everybody else. Of course I am acquainted with them all. But to tell you the truth, other writers tend to make me nervous.

Yael Medini

Not Undelighted

*For more than a year I had been threatening, as much in jest as in earnest, to "interview" Yael Medini, a writer who also happens to be a cousin and friend. Several years before, I had in a very minor way helped to smooth a path for the English-language publication of "Savta," a touching memoir she had written about her maternal grandmother (*Midstream, *January 1985). Then in 1987 Yael published a collection of short stories,* Hacavalier Sheli [My Cavalier], *the title story of which was "Savta" under an alias.*

Was cousinage sufficient cause not *to follow through on my threat? What sheer perversity! The fact was that, although we had seen each other intermittently for much of the decade I had lived in Israel, there were both general concerns and biographical matters about which I was curious but had never seen appropriate to ask. What fitter occasion than a formal interview could possibly be contrived? And to whom better than Yael should fall the honor of being the 18th conversation, capstone for* We Are All Close, *the writer whom I had known the longest and with whom I was myself by far the closest?*

It was late on a March afternoon in 1988; the rainy winter seemed finally in full retreat. I arrived at Yael's comfortable home on a quiet street in a suburb of Tel Aviv after a day's outing with Yishai, my 10-year-old son. As we sat together in Ramat Gan, 8,000 miles away Yitzhak Shamir was conferring with George Shultz, and 30 minutes away Israeli teenagers in uniform were confronting Palestinian teenagers in kaffiyehs. The walls of the living and dining rooms were covered with paintings and prints. Mementos and photos of her father, Israel's second Prime Minister, were also prominently in evidence.

Yael is in her mid-50s. Her husband, Gidon, an American-born psychologist at Tel Aviv University, arrived while we were seated at the dining room table and my pen was flying over sheets of paper. They have three grown children, and we were all looking forward to becoming first-time grandparents in the early summer. Although Yael does not speak rapidly, she proceeded with so little hesitation that several times I had to rein in the flow to give my hand a chance to catch up.

Haim Chertok: You were saying that you thought this is a particularly good period to be a woman writer.

Yael Medini: Oh, I think a very good time indeed. You see, I consider myself a quite marginal figure on the Israeli literary scene. However, just because I am a woman, willy-nilly my writing is seen as an expression of feminism. I speak for a Cause.

HC: Well, *hasn't* being a woman played a significant factor in your writing?

YM [laughing]: Certainly. Had I been a man, I would have had to be more concerned about making a living, and I would have written even less.

HC: I rather doubt that.

YM: But it's true! Haim, as a suburban housewife, all these years I have been a kept woman—a very well-kept woman—and so I have had the time to write. It's difficult for me to imagine how many of the male writers do in fact manage to work full-time and write as much as they do.

Did you know that next week I have been invited to participate with three other writers in a performance at *Beit Hasofer* in Tel Aviv? We will be interviewed by Carmit Guy [television newswoman].

HC: Well, perhaps our conversation can serve as a good preliminary. But wait! Aren't you being invited primarily because *Hacavalier Sheli* has recently appeared rather than that you are a woman writer?

YM: I'm not all that sure. One reviewer talked mainly about my stories' lacking sufficient impact. For all I know, he may be correct. But another example: there is shortly to be published in London a collection of short stories by Israeli *women* writers. Nilli Cohen, the Director at the Institute for the Translation of Hebrew Literature . . . do you know her?

HC: Yes, certainly.

YM: She submitted several stories from my collection.

HC: Your *new* collection?

YM [laughing]: My *only* collection. I just call it "the collection." Anyway, I just learned that they are debating between "The Music Competition" and "My Cavalier," which, as you know, is about my grandmother.

HC: Why did you change its homely name?

YM: Oh, I thought that whereas in Hebrew the word *savta* sounds mundane, in English the word carries a special flavor. The new title comes from the ironical way my grandma referred to her husband, which is also one of the major themes of her life.

"The Music Competition" is a story I'm particularly fond of. It concerns a young girl who must decide between making her life and career in music together with her much older piano teacher, with all that connotes, or by risking everything—sinking or swimming—in pursuit of a career without him. [Smiles] It's a funny thing, I have rewritten that story on several different occasions, and each time I've provided it with a new ending. I am sure this has less to do with the girl in the story than with where I happen to be in my own life.

HC: Oh? How does it end most recently?

YM: She abandons her talent, gives up her career entirely. It is too heavy, too overwhelming a burden for her to carry throughout her life. She would rather be an everyday, plain person. But you know, the thing I really fear that readers would not understand is that my real point is not abnegation but rather that, in reality, there are no "everyday, plain persons." [Smiles] This final choice may be a product of more mature reflection or experience, but I'm not sure it is best for the story.

As for the London editors having to choose between these two stories, I am, let me say, not undelighted.

HC: I like your third choice, but whatever you do, please don't plague the reader with all three options. I'm not fond of fiction that draws such attention to itself as artifice.

YM: Perhaps you are right. Anyway, such an artificial contrivance as a volume of short stories by Israelis who are women was unthought-of even a few years ago. It's very nice for me, of course, but you know, though the stories are very special to me, and I am satisfied that they are the best I can do, I agree with the critics who think they are not all *that* special as stories. What I mean is that I can think of quite a few fine Israeli writers that happen not to be women who are these days not getting such nice letters from London. So you see, we live in a time when being a writer who is also a woman has its attractive aspects.

HC: I just finished doing a review of some novels that the Jewish Publication Society has reissued. Very fine books, among which is one called *Wasteland.* It first appeared in 1946. The writer is "Jo Sinclair," the penname Ruth Seid took so that *Esquire* would consider printing her work.

YM: They sent me a copy of the translations from London. At first reading, they seemed to me, as the expression goes in Hebrew, like good "first plowings"—too candid, too exact. But that initial reaction was like the shock you get when you see an unexpected reflection of your own image. On successive readings, I realized how fine the translations actually were. The translator, Philip Simpson, had managed translations that were literary—poetic but usually quite accurate. I was more than a little surprised. You see, my own Hebrew is not especially poetic. I generally adhere to plain, unmetaphorical, everyday language. Not as a matter of principle; it's just the way I write. I also shy away from anything overblown or shmaltzy.

However, I find the problem of dealing with multiple connotations really interesting. Inevitably, there are places where the Hebrew word carries simultaneous meanings, and one gets misplaced in translation. This can be very painful. At one point in "The Music Competition," I described the sun going down. You know here in Israel we have hardly any twilight at all. One minute there's daylight; then suddenly night has fallen. Someone once told me that the absence of twilight was the reason we Israelis see things in such black and white terms. Who knows? The young woman can't get enough of the light, and then the sun sinks, swallowed by the sea, which I wrote as *histalek*. The sound of this in Hebrew has a light touch, but yet it also suggests death. I wanted both qualities. In English it sounded all wrong. I think Simpson used the word "departs" or "departure."

HC: But "depart" can carry overtones of death in English as well as just "to leave."

YM: I suppose, but it's still too heavy. The lightness I wanted also has . . . departed.

HC: I wonder whether women writers are fussier about translating their work than are men. Shulamith Hareven, whose translator is not some *yored* but Hillel Halkin, also complains that translation undoes many of her best effects.

YM: I'm sure that she's right. Even though we can learn a lot from translations, I always read English-language works in the original. Lately I've been trying to do that with French, mostly by every day reading a few pages of a novel. I just love the sound of it. I fear that in this life, however, no additional foreign languages will ever get completely housebroken.

Back in 1959, I translated Carson McCullers' *The Heart Is a Lonely Hunter* into Hebrew. It was for me a very difficult task; in fact, I don't think I would ever do anything like that again. Nevertheless, I did feel that I had entered the very body and breath of the author: every word, every paragraph I relived. Among other things, a work of literature is a wedding of content and garment, and sometimes the translator can be *un haut couturier.* On balance, however, it isn't necessarily true that a work of literature must suffer in translation. Despite our stylistic differences, I think Simpson managed to be true to the spirit of my story.

HC: Wasn't that a Hebrew edition of Joyce's *Ulysses* that I saw in the bedroom?

YM: Yes, but I'm not reading it. One of my children's friends left it here. By the way, "Simpson" may not sound particularly Jewish, but I wouldn't jump to the conclusion that he's necessarily an ex-Israeli wearing linguistic disguise. [Pause] I never use the word *yored* any more. Here is your coffee.

HC: Thank you. I'm curious: at what point in your life were you when first you wrote "The Music Competition"?

YM: Oh, I can tell almost exactly. We were taking a trip to Eilat and on to Sharm-el-Sheikh on the Sinai coast. [Smiles] This was still in the days of our Israeli Empire, and Yamli, our youngest—she must then have been about seven—was with us. I remember looking at her and thinking, "What will she do in her life? With her life?" When I reread the story I had written, I was genuinely moved by the predicament of the young woman musician, by her desire for excellence . . . and by the emotion that generated it.

HC: It might be useful for you to recount all that you have written.

YM: It won't take very long. My first book, published in 1960, I'm almost ashamed of. It was a book of poems, quatrains to be exact, based upon the letters of the Hebrew alphabet. I originally contrived it for Yotam, our son, then a little boy. What I'm embarrassed about is that while I just may well be a writer, a poet I am assuredly not. Writing the little four-line poems seemed so easy, but just being facile with rhymes, even for a children's book, really isn't enough. I would not write it again.

HC: When did your first book for adults appear?

YM: That was in 1977: *Kavim V'Kashtot* [*Arcs and Traces*]. I like the title, which I got from my neighbor up the street. She's a lecturer at Bar-Ilan University.

I think of this novel as embodying the dilemma of vicarious living. The heroine must determine whether she is ready to begin living her own life: to pay the price of authenticity and to stand being enriched by its remunerations. The novel grew almost of its own accord out of a short story that had won special recognition in a contest organized by *Keshet* [prominent literary periodical]. Later they published it. I've been told that novels should not grow out of short stories, but this one seemed determined to.

Now, although I have been writing and publishing stories in periodicals all through these years, last year's collection is only my third book.

HC: When did you actually begin your writing?

YM: It was when I was studying at Hunter College on Sixty-eighth Street in Manhattan. I had had a difficult time writing when I was younger, during my school years in Palestine. Both my teachers and my father were very strict and demanding. A composition would be returned with every possible error prominently marked; my father's usual reaction would be praise for the teacher for being so thorough! The best mark I ever received on a composition was an "Almost Good" [C+]. I felt I could never satisfy them, and felt rather imposed upon.

I recall—I was twelve or thirteen so it was around 1943—that I was assigned to write about any wish I wanted to come true. There is a legend that on the night of *Shavuot* [Pentecost], such wishes may be granted. At the time, my older brother Kobi wanted nothing more in the world than to own a certain bicycle. We children were never given pocket money, but he saved all the money that relatives had given him, his *Hanukkah gelt* [money], and then what little he could earn. Once our aunt gave him a whole shilling. That was then a princely sum. Little by little, the sum mounted. So I wrote a composition wishing the bicycle for my brother.

My teacher's response is unforgettable: "Is this an appropriate wish for the daughter of the Director of Foreign Affairs of the Jewish Agency?" [Laughs] Sometimes I think that maybe the teacher was right after all, that I'm still an Almost Good.

HC: I know better, but with your fit for self-deprecation, perhaps it is well you're so well-kept. How long in all did you live in the States?

YM· About seven years. After such a strict early education, Hunter proved a liberating experience for me. I naturally gravitated toward the Liberal Arts and a group of instructors who were all earnest, austere, most of them unmarried, and not Jewish. What they conveyed along with their subjects was a sense of integrity. The Shakespeare course that Professor Gatch offered us really was so good, so rewarding that even after all these years, it stands as one of the richest experiences of my life. She really opened up Shakespeare for me.

I took a Creative Writing course there which significantly affected my life. There were only twelve of us in the class, among whom was one other foreign-born student, a very bright girl from Poland. Not Jewish, I think. Our first theme was on "My Room," and I labored so hard to make it good! When I read it aloud, the teacher laughed . . . but in all the right places. Unlike my grade school teachers, she did not circle every error; instead, she praised whatever was good. We moved on to "My Street," and then to an account of "A Person in My Family"— my paternal grandmother—which proved a big hit.

Meanwhile the Polish girl, she was very bright and energetic—a little like a young Shulamith Hareven—had started a new literary newspaper. She asked me to submit a story, so I wrote the one about a kibbutz experince. It was printed. That was the first time that I felt I could write.

HC: How long did you live on a kibbutz?

YM: Only for one year, 1949–50. At the time, it was expected and natural for young people of my background to spend some time on a kibbutz. Kibbutzim embody wonderful ideals and values, but it was soon plain that the style of living really did not suit me.

HC [after a phone interruption]: You've written a good deal about your family, especially, it seems, your grandmothers. What about your famous father?

YM: In some guises, bits and pieces of my father hover in the background of some of the autobiographical stories where I draw on facets of him which afford me some pleasure. If I don't feel up to an *en face* portrait, it's due not so much to his strong impact as to the simple fact of his having been my father. This, after all, seems to me quite natural. To come to terms in one's lifetime with one's parents is no mean feat. I, for one, would need another life to grapple with him on paper. But then there's the miracle of "literary ecology": I write about your father; you write about mine.

I have, however, also written five autobiographical stories that are still unpublished. In some of them I string some reminiscences in which he plays a prominent part along a thread of plot in order to construct the narrative. (The heroine of one of them, by the way, is my old nanny. That was her just before on the telephone. She is now really quite old.) One story concerns my father and an Arab. The conversation proceeds in Arabic, and my father does the translating. My older brother has read these stories. His feeling is that they fall between the two chairs of story and documentary. Nevertheless, they had been accepted for publication by *Sifra'ut Hapoalim* [a publisher].

Last week, however, I met with one of their editors, and she now wants me to add a sixth story, "A Literary Case," which revolves around a literary debate. It's based on an actual situation and deals with Zionist idealism—work, the land, making do with less—and the problem of which ideals to believe in and to follow. But the editor also wants certain revisions. To tell you the truth, the whole business needs mulling over. It may still be too soon or too problematic to publish these stories.

HC: Earlier you mentioned that you refrain from using the term *yored*. Because it's disparaging?

YM: That's right. I don't attach any judgment to a person's decision where to settle. Regarding Israel, there is, as you know, a pull, but there is also a push. I think it has always been so. I get particularly angry at how the Israeli establishment relates to ex-

Israelis in the United States. Those who succeed are called "big givers," but the ones who are struggling have the additional burden of being labeled *yordim*. I abhor such a double standard.

The right thing, I think, is to employ a humane approach that takes full and fair account of personal motivation and human values. Moreover, it's simply stupid to stigmatize all those former Israelis, to alienate them and their children from us. [Smiles] Maybe it's just one of our more minor mistakes. Neither, by the way, do I like the word *oleh* for an immigrant. It seems to me too flowery.

HC: I know what you mean. What I especially recoil at is the use of *hozer b'tshuva* for someone who has decided to observe the *mitzvot*. It exudes falseness, and it has nothing to do with me. But what other "mistakes" might you have in mind?

YM: I am not a historian, but something very troublesome is currently afflicting us in Israel. It has been for some time. It seems to me that in the period after Herzl, the Zionist movement threw up several generations of remarkably gifted, dynamic personalities. Each era, each crisis demanded action, and then and there the nucleus emerged, exercising true leadership.

However, the events from the 1920s to the '40s were so tremendous and exhilarating that something seemed to peak or crest just as we finally won our struggle for statehood and independence. It's as if the flood of events and the long shadow of their great predecessors left my generation depleted, exhausted. We have not been able to rise to meet Israel's new challenges.

Signs of it are everywhere. A simple example is our *Kupat Holim* [Health Insurance Fund]. At the start its goals were humane, egalitarian, life-serving: it was an expression of our basic values. Now it is very largely a self-serving instrument, a vast bureaucracy that cannot evolve, adapt, or meet new challenges. As a result, our entire health system is collapsing.

It's the same with all our structures—education, the army,

everything. Consider women in the army. It was born out of the ethos of the pioneering days. And at the time, the women served a genuinely vital role. I think that today—indeed, these days in particular—many women really don't feel a close identification to the mission of the state. Though my own daughter's recent experience as a soldier–teacher was highly successful, speaking generally, I can't help but think much time and money are wasted.

HC: I can't agree with you. For many of the girls from outlying areas, the army still represents an opportunity to broaden their perspectives. And from the other direction, we have serving in Yeroham a wonderful group of young women soldiers, most from Jerusalem, who are members of a *nahal* unit [combining military service and pioneering].

YM: Yes, it could be that you are right about the girls from and in development towns.

HC: How do you relate to our current political impasse and the Palestinian uprising in the territories?

YM: It is very difficult. By nature, I am an optimist. There are so many things in life which I'm involved with and which I enjoy that I tend to think that things must get better. But we are now living through a time of such violence, cruelty, and fascistic apparitions that I feel vast inner pain. What is happening in the territories today is horrific.

When I write letters to people overseas, I find myself apologizing for my very well-being. After all, I and my family *are* all well. Yet there is such a gap between us and the situation just a few miles to the south and east. I end up writing something like "all is well in my house." It is easy enough for my friends to read between the lines.

HC: Though this is a time of depleted national leadership, how would you assess the present moment in Israeli literature?

YM: Ah, that *is* something else. I often feel energized by how many good books are now being written here. Lately, I've been

reading some very fine new novels: *Married Life* by David Fogel
and *Golem in Circle*—it's about a pianist—by Lily Perry-Amitai.
And last week we saw a dramatization of Haim Be'er's *Notzot*. It
was really wonderful. They are all part of the recent tremendous
surge of talent in Israel.

More and more nowadays people seem to be drawn to the arts.
Perhaps the explanation is really quite simple. During Israel's
heroic period, it was more difficult to criticize the contemporary
scene because identification with it was so powerful. Also, the
social scene was really quite clean and healthy. There was precious little corruption or decadence. Literature, which has a
strong tendency to be critical, had much less to grasp at or
to attach itself to. I remember in the Sixties when I first read
Agnon's *Shirah*. It was set in the Thirties. Its hero is a professor;
it was all right to put *him* on the operating table. But then it was
very interesting for me to see how, in a marginal scene, Agnon
portrayed in satirical fashion a personality who in some ways re-
sembled my father. It was quite well done.

And now, when things are so bad, we have such a fertile period
for writers. Lately, there have been whole series of apocalyptic
and futuristic novels—fantasies, really—by writers like Amos
Keinan, Benjamin Tammuz, and Yitzhak Ben-Ner. I like very
much Meir Agasi's *The Black Hills of Dakota* . . .

HC: . . . of Dakota!

YM: Yes, but it's not about your Dakota. It depicts life in a kibbutz in the Fifties. It is a very honest, not very complimentary
presentation.

HC: How do you feel about, of all things, Judaism?

YM: My answer may not be a precise response to your question.
What I *can* say is that I have always felt that the best of all possible fates for a person was to be a Jew living in the State of
Israel. [Pause] I must qualify this, however, with the pain I feel
at present when I think of the diminished imagination of our national leadership, of our government's unwillingness to compro-

mise for the sake of peace, and of the spirit of dogmatism now so common in the land.

HC: Yael, thank you very much.

YM: The "interview" is over? Good. Now I can think about serving some dinner to you and to Yishai. You must be hungry after your day on the town. And then we can talk!

*Photographs on pages 10, 25, 63, 165, 183
copyright by Mark W. Berghash, 20/20 Services Inc.*

*Photograph on page 49 copyright by Mark W. Berghash,
20/20 Services Inc.
Courtesy Marcuse Pfeifer Gallery*

Photograph on page 75 copyright by Yael Avi-Yona

Photograph on page 149 by Jerry Bauer